Englisches Schülertheater - Black Comedy

Kinder-, Schul- und Jugendtheater
Beiträge zu Theorie und Praxis

Herausgegeben von Charlotte Oberfeld
und Heiko Kauffmann

Band 4

Verlag Peter Lang
Frankfurt am Main · Bern · New York · Paris

Daniel Meyer-Dinkgräfe

Englisches Schülertheater – Black Comedy

Theorie und Praxis
einer englischsprachigen
Theater-Arbeitsgemeinschaft
in der gymnasialen Oberstufe

Verlag Peter Lang
Frankfurt am Main · Bern · New York · Paris

CIP-Titelaufnahme der Deutschen Bibliothek

Meyer-Dinkgräfe, Daniel:

Englisches Schülertheater - Black comedy : Theorie u. Praxis e.
englischsprach. Theater-Arbeitsgemeinschaft in d. gymnasialen
Oberstufe / Daniel Meyer-Dinkgräfe. - Frankfurt am Main ; Bern ;
New York ; Paris : Lang, 1988
    (Kinder-, Schul- und Jugendtheater ; Bd. 4)
    ISBN 3-8204-0994-7

NE: GT

ISSN 0723-8312
ISBN 3-8204-0994-7

© Verlag Peter Lang GmbH, Frankfurt am Main 1988

Printed in Germany

VORWORT

Die vorliegende Arbeit ist die erweiterte Fassung der
Schriftlichen Hausarbeit für das Lehramt für die Sekundarstufe II am Studienseminar Krefeld II.

Ich danke den Teilnehmern der Theater-AG für ihr großes
Interesse und Engagement. Der Direktorin des Ricarda-Huch-
Gymnasiums, Krefeld, Frau Dr. Stephan-Kühn, danke ich für
die Unterstützung bei der Durchführung der Theater-AG.
Frau Prof. Charlotte Oberfeld danke ich für die Aufnahme der
Arbeit in ihre Reihe "Kinder-, Schul- und Jugendtheater".

Daniel Meyer-Dinkgräfe, Grevenbroich 2, September 1987

INHALTSÜBERSICHT

ANHANG

1

I. THEATER UND SCHULE

Eine "gezielte pädagogische Inanspruchnahme des Theaterspielens"[1] läßt sich in Deutschland bereits vom 16. Jahrhundert an
nachweisen. Zweck des lateinischen Schuldramas im 16. und 17.
Jahrhundert war

Übung in der Anwendung der lateinischen Sprache, Stärkung des
Gedächtnisses, Wiederholung des biblischen und geschichtlichen
Lehrstoffes, lehrhafte Vorführung der Belohnung guter und Be-
strafung schlechter Taten.[2]

Auch "Übung in der Kunst der Rede und die Gewöhnung an freies
und ungezwungenes Auftreten vor größerer Menschenmenge"[3] wurden
angestrebt. Die weitere Entwicklung verlief über das Jesuiten-
theater im 17. Jahrhundert, die Lesedramen des Christian Felix
Weisse in der aufklärerischen Pädagogik des 18. Jahrhunderts bis
hin zu dem Aufschwung des Laienspiels im Rahmen der deutschen
Jugendbewegung im ersten Drittel dieses Jahrhunderts.[4]

Nach 1945 wurde das Laienspiel wieder aufgenommen. Gleichzei-
tig bemühte man sich um die gezielte Integration des Theater-
spieles in der Schule.[5] In den ersten Jahren überwogen bei der
Untersuchung der pädagogischen Möglichkeiten von Theater in der
Schule "musisch-ästhetisch akzentuierende Ansätze"[6], die bei
der

Bestimmung der pädagogischen Bedeutung, des Lehr- und Lern-
wertes des darstellenden Spiels meist über die Mitteilung
von Erlebniswerten oder über bildungsphilosophisch orientier-
te, allgemeine Wertzuschreibungen nicht hinausgelangt waren.[7]

Eher pädagogisch-lerntheoretisch ausgerichtete Ansätze finden
sich dagegen mit Beginn der siebziger Jahre. Die Reform der gymnasialen Oberstufe in der Sekundarstufe II, eingeleitet durch
die "Vereinbarung zur Neugestaltung der gymnasialen Oberstufe in
der Sekundarstufe II" der Kultusministerkonferenz am 7.7.1972[8],
brachte Überlegungen zur Einbeziehung eines Theaterfaches in den
Fächerkanon der Oberstufe mit sich. Im Laufe der Entwicklung er-

gaben sich von Bundesland zu Bundesland unterschiedliche Regelungen.[9] In Nordrhein-Westfalen beispielsweise kann "darstellendes Spiel" im Rahmen eines maximal zweisemestrigen Literaturgrundkurses (auch in einer Fremdsprache) angeboten werden.[10]

Im Zuge dieser Neuorientierung kam es auch zu einer Änderung der Fachtermini. Kluge stellte diesbezüglich folgende Nomenklatur auf:

Darstellendes Spiel wird heute als Ober- oder Sammelbegriff akzeptiert, dem eine Reihe gestaltender, nachgestaltender oder medienorientierter Spielformen zugeordnet werden.[11]

Im einzelnen sind dies:

1) Vorgeformt, textgebunden, nachgestaltend: Schulbühnenspiel, Textspiel.

2) Improvisierend, Text erarbeitend, gestaltend: Stegreifspiel, Xselbsterarbeitetes Spiel.

3) Improvisierend, non-verbal, gestaltend: Pantomime, Scharade.

4) Vorgeformt/improvisiert, textgebunden/textunabhängig, medienorientiert: Maskenspiel, Puppenspiel, Marionettenspiel.

Auch diese Terminologie hat sicherlich ihre Problematik - die Unterscheidung von Textspiel und Schulbühnenspiel leuchtet beispielsweise nicht ganz ein. Jede Untersuchung zu Theater in der Schule muß daher eine genaue Schwerpunktbeschreibung und -legitimation liefern.

Für fast alle Auswirkungen von Schülertheater im pädagogischen Bereich gilt, daß es sich um Annahmen und Vermutungen handelt, für die im einzelnen - obschon einige von ihnen unmittelbar einleuchtend erscheinen mögen - weder sichere empirische Belege noch ausreichende lerntheoretische Begründungen vorliegen.[12]

Dies trifft insbesondere für den Spracherwerb in einer Fremdsprache, hier Englisch, durch Einstudierung eines fremdsprachigen Dramas mit dem Ziel der Schulaufführung zu: "Über fremdsprachiges Schülertheater, dessen wird man sich nach kurzer Suche ge-

wahr, ist nicht viel in Erfahrung zu bringen"[13], heißt es noch
Anfang 1986 in einem Aufsatz der Fachzeitschrift Die Neueren
Sprachen.

Ich möchte nun im Rahmen dieser Arbeit versuchen, zweierlei
zu leisten: zum einen soll zumindest ansatzweise eine lerntheoretische Begründung für den Einsatz von englischsprachigem Schul-
theater für den Spracherwerb Englisch vorgestellt werden. Dabei
gehe ich auf die Spracherwerbsforschung ein und stelle den Zusammenhang von "Theaterarbeit" im Rahmen der Schule und Spracherwerb
her. Dies Kapitel ist in seinen Ausführungen nicht streng auf ein
bestimmtes einzustudierendes englisches Drama ausgerichtet. Hin-
weise auf Shaffers Black Comedy dienen der Veranschaulichung der
allgemeinen Überlegungen. Zum anderen möchte ich Methoden und
Mittel vorstellen, die mir zum Erreichen meiner Ziele im Bereich
des englischen Spracherwerbs als sinnvoll erscheinen. Dies Kapitel erhält die Form eines Praxisberichts und bezieht sich auf die
konkrete Erarbeitung von Shaffers Black Comedy in der Theater-AG
der Oberstufe des Ricarda-Huch-Gymnasiums in Krefeld, meiner Aus-
bildungsschule im Referendariat.

Zunächst beginne ich mit theoretischen und didaktischen Überlegungen zum Spracherwerb Englisch durch fremdsprachiges Schülertheater. Als Rahmen für die Ausführungen dieses Kapitels wähle
ich die Lernbereiche, die die Richtlinien Englisch für die gymnasiale Oberstufe NRW in dem unten abgebildeten Diagramm schema-
tisch verdeutlichen. Im zweiten Teil folgt der Praxisbericht, der
die Lern- und Lehrvoraussetzungen, sowie Planung und Durchführung
der Probenarbeit enthält.

II. SPRACHERWERB DURCH THEATER -
THEORETISCHE UND DIDAKTISCHE ÜBERLEGUNGEN

Die Schüler der englischen Theater-AG des Ricarda-Huch-Gymnasiums in Krefeld hatten bereits zwei Einakter von Alan Ayckbourn, A Talk in the Park und Mother Figure, einstudiert und gespielt. Nun wollten sie ein längeres Stück eines anderen Autors. Ich habe aus meiner Kenntnis des zeitgenössischen englischen Dramas Peter Shaffers Einakter Black Comedy ausgewählt.[14] Im folgenden möchte ich analysieren, inwiefern sich gerade auch dieser Text für die Umsetzung in einer Theater-AG eignet. Dabei beziehe ich mich auf die für den Spracherwerb Englisch fachspezifischen Lernziele und -bereiche, wie sie in dem oben abgebildeten Diagramm dargestellt sind. Die Reihenfolge wird von der Themenstellung der Arbeit bestimmt:

1) Sprachbeherrschung.
2) Wissen über Sprache.
3) Textrezeption und Textproduktion.
4) Wissen über Textarten.
5) Wissen über Sender und Adressaten.
6) Methodenbeherrschung.
7) Haltungen und Einstellungen.
8) Auswirkungen im Bereich des Englischunterrichts.
9) Lernerfolgskontrolle.

1. Sprachbeherrschung

Einige Autoren vertreten die Ansicht, Stegreifspiel in der Fremdsprache sei "für die Schüler leichter und lustvoller (...) als das gebundene Spiel".[15] Sie fragen sich, "ob der sprachliche Gewinn bei feststehendem Text wirklich größer ist".[16] Daher gilt es zunächst zu begründen, warum ich für die Arbeit in der Theater-AG eine literarische Vorlage zum Nachvollzug ausgewählt habe. Die genannten Autoren gehen in ihrer Argumentation für den Übergang von textgebundenem zu textfreiem darstellenden Spiel vom Englischunterricht in der Schule aus.[17] Auf den Englischunterricht läßt sich sicherlich Amtmanns Feststellung zu darstellendem Spiel im Unterricht allgemein übertragen: "Spiel im Unterricht ist möglich in zeitlich begrenzten Kleinformen, die sich in den Unterricht einfügen."[18] Ob im Rahmen von Englischunterricht das Stegreifspiel zur besseren Sprachbeherrschung vielleicht wirkungsvoller beiträgt, als die zeitlich umfangreichere Erarbeitung eines vorgegebenen Textes, kann Thema einer eigenständigen Untersuchung sein. In einer Theater-Arbeitsgemeinschaft ist jedoch viel mehr Zeit vorhanden, als im Englischunterricht, da dieser nicht in der vollen Stundenzahl dem darstellenden Spiel gewidmet werden kann. Die in der Theater-AG vorhandene Zeit sollte daher dadurch ausgenutzt werden, daß ein vorgegebener Text für die Bühne erarbeitet wurde.

Bulmer bringt ein weiteres Argument für den Nachvollzug einer Textvorlage: "It is asking a lot to concentrate on movement, gesture, facial expression, and inventing dialogue at the same time."[19] Der Schüler wird möglicherweise durch Stegreifspiel in der Fremdsprache überfordert. Wenn man sich mit diesen Argumenten für einen vorgegebenen Text und gegen das Stegreifspiel entscheidet, folgt die Frage, ob es eine Vorlage sein sollte, die von den Schülern selbst erarbeitet, also selbst geschrieben wurde, oder um einen literarischen Text. Black Comedy ist ein zeitgenössisches englisches Drama, es wurde am 27.7.1965 vom National Theatre in Chichester uraufgeführt.[20] Die Sprache der Figuren ist modernes, grammatisch korrektes Englisch. Obwohl das Stück sprachlich nicht übermäßig anspruchsvoll ist, repräsentiert es doch eine Sprachebene, die komplexer und idiomatischer ist, als ein von den Schülern selbst geschriebener Text es sein könnte. Die Schüler verfügen nicht über die Ausdrucksmittel eines englischen Dramatikers. Durch die komplexe Sprachstruktur der literarischen Vorlage lernen die Schüler mehr, als durch einen selbst verfaßten Text beziehungsweise den Vorgang der Texterstellung.

Diese These möchte ich im folgenden durch Überlegungen stützen, die auf der Zweitsprachenerwerbstheorie von Krashen beruhen.

Stephen Krashen unterscheidet zwischen language acquisition und language learning. Language acquisition ist ein natürlicher, unbewußter Vorgang des Spracherwerbs, der dann einsetzt, wenn der Lerner mit der Zielsprache in Kontakt kommt. Die genaueren Vorgänge, die dabei ablaufen, ähneln denen des Erstsprachenerwerbs beim Kind.[21] Language learning dagegen ist ein bewußter Vorgang, der auf formalem Lernen beruht und daher, im Gegensatz zu language acquisition, beeinflußbar ist. Um language acquisition zu gewährleisten, gilt es, eine sprachliche Umgebung zu schaffen, die so genau wie möglich mit authentischen kommunikativen Gegebenheiten der Zielsprache übereinstimmt:[22]

Learners have to be given the opportunity to make their own subconscious selections of items to be acquired, based on what they individually find communicatively useful at each stage of their development.[23]

Bei der Einstudierung eines englischen Dramas wie Black Comedy wird den Schülern in zweifacher Hinsicht die Gelegenheit zu language acquisition geboten:

a) Die Proben erfolgen in englischer Sprache. Die Situation ist also echt: Gemeinsam diskutieren die Schüler untereinander und mit mir, wie das Stück sprachlich, gestisch, mimisch usw. gestaltet werden soll. Besonders in einer Farce wie Black Comedy ist die Koordination von Gängen, Bewegungen und Sprache sehr wichtig: "The action requires split-second timing (...)."[24] Es wird daher einiger Diskussionen bedürfen, um dieses "timing" zu erarbeiten. Die Echtheit der Kommunikation in englischer Sprache steht im Gegensatz zum eher künstlichen Charakter englischsprachiger Kommunikationssituationen im Englischunterricht. Die Echtheit wird in der Situation der Theater-AG nur dadurch getrübt, daß Englisch nicht notwendigerweise die Kommunikationssprache ist.

b) Black Comedy stellt trotz der farcenhaften Zuspitzung der Situationen realistische Figuren dar, die auf einer sprachlich authentischen Ebene miteinander sprechen. Eine gewisse Echtheit ist damit auch gegeben.

Beide Sprechsituationen, die weitgehend echte der englischsprachigen Probenarbeit (auf niedrigerer sprachlicher Ebene als das Drama) und die als Kommunikationssituation weniger echte, gespielte Authentizität von Black Comedy (auf höherer sprachlicher Ebene als die Probensprache),stellen unterschiedlich akzentuierte Gelegenheiten für die Schüler dar, im Sinne der language acquisition unbewußt Sprachmaterial aufzunehmen. Eine von den Schülern verfaßte Textvorlage wäre sprachlich nicht wesentlich komplexer und idiomatischer als die Ebene, die die Schüler bei der Probenarbeit in englischer Sprache erreichen können. Gerade auch deshalb ist eine literarische Vorlage wie Black Comedy, also sprachlich anspruchsvoller als die eigene Sprachebene der Schüler, aber nicht überfordernd, für optimale language acquisition sinnvoll.

Das Element, das language acquisition und language learning verbindet und der Theorie von Krashen ihren Namen gegeben hat, ist die Monitor-Funktion des learned system gegenüber dem acquired system:

> Speech is initiated by the acquired system. The learned system does not initiate speech. It may only apply after speech has been initiated by the acquired system, i.e. somewhere "before" the actual verbalization. The learned system is said to monitor,i.e. to modify, the output by the acquired system towards greater grammatical correctness. In this respect, the monitor can be likened to an editing device.[25]

Krashen geht dabei davon aus, daß kein Transfer vom learned system zum acquired system erfolgt. Das learned system dient ausschließlich der Monitorfunktion.[26] Die Erfahrung widerspricht jedoch der Annahme dieser Unmöglichkeit eines Transfers.[27] Ellis

kommt daher zu folgender Erweiterung von Krashens Theorie:
"It may be that communicative opportunity is necessary as a
switch that starts the flow of learnt to acquired knowledge."[28]
Seine Schlußfolgerung ist, daß informelle kommunikative Ansätze
des Zweitsprachenerwerbs eine doppelte Funktion erfüllen: sie
ermöglichen

a) Language acquisition, indem sie Gelegenheiten zu
   Kommunikation schaffen;

b) einen Transfer vom learned system auf das acquired system.

Die Einstudierung von Black Comedy erfüllt als infomeller kommu-
nikativer Ansatz in Ellis'Sinne die beiden genannten Funktionen.

Language acquisition kann im einzelnen in folgenden Bereichen
erfolgen:

a) Grammatische Richtigkeit

   Diese ist in Black Comedy gegeben. Bei der englischsprachigen
Probenarbeit wird ebenfalls auf grammatische Richtigkeit der Äuße-
rungen geachtet; Verbesserungen erfolgen durch andere Schüler
oder durch mich.

b) Aussprache

   Vor einem Theaterpublikum, das sonst nicht unbedingt daran gewöhnt ist, hier in Deutschland englisches Theater zu sehen, ist
eine richtige, besonders klare und deutliche Aussprache erforderlich. Die Teilnahme von Schülern in der Theater-AG, die längere
Zeit im englischsprachigen Ausland waren, wird sich hier günstig
auswirken.

c) Intonation

Es geht hier insbesondere darum, das bei den Schülern beim
Vorlesen englischer Dialoge oft zu bemerkende Leiern zu verhin-
dern, das der realistischen Intonation, die angestrebt wird, nicht
entspricht. Bulmer führt aus:

Learning to act in a foreign language means, in addition,
concentrating on those most neglected areas of language
learning, namely: intonation, register and rhythm, which are
often, more so than incorrect pronunciation, the cause of
miscommunication.[29]

d) Lexikalisch-semantischer Bereich

In der Probenarbeit wird theater- und darstellungsbezogenes
Vokabular verwendet und gegebenenfalls erklärend eingeführt,
etwa die Einteilung der Bühne in upstage, downstage, centrestage,
jeweils left, middle, right. Auch die intensive Beschäftigung mit
dem Dramentext, die notwendig ist, um den Text sinngebend zu
spielen, macht mit neuen Vokabeln bekannt. Die motivierende
Situation der Theaterarbeit in der Fremdsprache erleichtert (als
spielerisches Lernen) die Aufnahme dieser Elemente in den aktiven
und passiven Wortschatz.

e) Leseverstehen

Wie bereits angedeutet, erfordert die Umsetzung eines Textes
auf der Bühne ein Lesen, das intensiver sein muß, als das im
Englischunterricht erforderliche: während bei der Lektüre von
literarischen Texten im Englischunterricht kursorisches und
statarisches Lesen abwechseln, liegt beim Lesen als Vorbereitung
auf darstellendes Spiel zwangsläufig eine statarische Lektüre vor.

f) Hörverstehen

Bei den in englischer Sprache gegebenen Regieanweisungen müssen die Schüler genau zuhören, um das Vorgestellte verstehen und
diskutieren zu können. Auch den Beiträgen der Mitschüler müssen
die Schüler zuhören. Dadurch, daß sie sich selbst um eine sinn-
vermittelnde Intonation bemühen müssen, etwa zur Darstellung
"emotionaler Implikationen einer Äußerung, wie sie sich auch in
Klangfarbe, Lautstärke und Sprechtempo manifestieren"[30], werden
sie für solche Intonationsnuancen in späteren Hörverstehenssitua-
tionen sensibilisiert. Das kann sich sowohl auf Theaterstücke,
Hörspiele und ähnliche "künstliche" Situationen beziehen, als
auch auf Situationen unter "realen Bedingungen der Kommunikation"[31]

2. Wissen über Sprache

Aus den obigen Ausführungen zum Lernbereich Sprachbeherrschung
lassen sich die folgenden Aspekte zu Wissen über Sprache ableiten:

a) Unterschiedliche Sprachmittel des Senders führen zu verschiedenen Eindrücken beziehungsweise Reaktionen beim Adressaten.
Dies gilt zunächst für die Kommunikation der Figuren in Black
Comedy untereinander, wie sie vom Autor im Text vorgegeben
ist. Sie muß von den Schülern erfaßt, nachvollzogen und ange-
messen dargestellt werden. Es gilt aber ebenso für die Wechsel-
wirkung von Schauspieler und Publikum: eine Äußerung, die im
Rahmen des Stückes ernst gemeint ist und ernst aufgefaßt wird,
kann beim Publikum aus verschiedenen Gründen als Anlaß zum
Lachen genommen werden. Schließlich ist noch die Kommunikationssituation der englischsprachigen Probenarbeit zu nennen.
Die Situation in Black Comedy ist völlig fiktiv. Die Schauspie-
ler-Publikum-Wechselwirkung vermittelt zwischen der Fiktionalität des Theaterstücks und der Realität der Anwesenheit der

Zuschauer im Theater. Die Kommunikationssituation der Probenarbeit schließlich enthält kein Element der Fiktionalität mehr.

b) In der Sprechsituation des Theaters ist eine besonders klare,
deutliche, adressatenbezogene Sprechweise erforderlich.

c) Die Figuren in Black Comedy sind als Typen gezeichnet; ein
Charakterisierungsmittel ist die Sprache. Als dümmliche De-
bütantin wird Carol Melkett durch die Verwendung des albern
wirkenden Suffix "-pegs" und durch die Redewendung "(...) is
laughingly known as (...)"[32] charakterisiert. Der deutsch-
stämmige Elektriker Schuppanzigh erinnert mit seiner gewählt-
philosophischen Sprache an das Klischee des Deutschen als
"Denker" - von einem Elektriker hingegen erwartet man eine
derartige Sprachebene nicht.[33] Dieser Kontrast wirkt komisch.
Colonel Melkett spricht knapp und zackig, wie man es von einem
Angehörigen des Militärs erwartet.[34] An dieser Stelle über-
schneidet sich der Lernbereich Wissen über Sprache mit dem zu
Wissen über Textarten, denn diese sprachliche Figurenzeichnung
ist typisch für die Textart Farce.

3. Textrezeption und Textproduktion

Die Textrezeption erfolgt durch intensives Lesen: zunächst
liest jeder Schüler den Text still für sich, oder auch für sich
allein laut. Spätestens auf den ersten Proben müssen die Schüler
laut lesen. Das Sprachsystem wird dadurch, und durch die beson-
dere, schon auf eine Re-produktion des Textes auf der Bühne hin
gelenkte Ausrichtung des Lesens (Was läuft ab? Mit welchen
sprachlichen Mitteln kann ich das am besten, am wirkungsvollsten,
umsetzen?) dem Schüler sehr deutlich. Besonderes Gewicht erhal-
ten die bereits erörterten Faktoren Intonation und Aussprache,
aber auch figurentypische Elemente der Sprache und solche des
lexikalisch-semantischen Bereichs.

Textproduktion ist im Falle der Einstudierung eines englischen Dramas die Re-Produktion eines vorgegebenen Textes. Doch die Probenarbeit ist ein kreatives Erarbeiten des Ausgangsmaterials; auch die Aufführung selbst bewegt sich zwar in vorgeformten, einstudierten Bahnen, sie erfordert jedoch einen jeweils neuen, kreativen Nachvollzug der Vorlage und ist somit weit mehr als "bloßes" Reproduzieren im Sinne eines Nachvollzugs ohne neue Komponenten.

In seinem Buch The Empty Space beschreibt der bekannte englische Regisseur Peter Brook, wie er die Kreativität des Schauspielers Paul Scofield erlebt:

It was as though the act of speaking a word sent through him vibrations that echoed back meanings more complex than his rational thinking could find; he would pronounce a word like "night", and then he would be compelled to pause: listening with all his being to the amazing impulses stirring in some mysterious inner chamber, he would experience the wonder of discovery at the moment when it happened. Those breaks, those sallies in depth, give his acting its absolutely personal structure of rhythms, its own instinctive meanings: to rehearse a part, he lets his whole nature, a milliard of supersensitive scanners, pass to and fro across the words. In performance the same process makes everything that he has apparently fixed come back again each night the same and absolutely different.[35)]

Diese Extremform schauspielerischer Kreativität kann und soll nicht Ziel der Schulbühne sein. Das Beispiel vermag aber sehr wohl zu erklären, weshalb die Produktion eines vorgelegten Textes auch dann noch mehr ist als "bloße" Reproduktion, wenn auch nur ein verschwindend kleiner Teil dessen realisiert wird, was Brook andeutet.

4. Wissen über Textarten - Black Comedy als Farce

Black Comedy ist eine Farce. Wenn auch die Gattung Farce in der Theater-AG nicht ausdrücklich zum theoretischen Gegenstand gemacht wird, wie dies bei der Behandlung einer Farce im Englischunterricht der Fall sein müßte (etwa bei der Behandlung der in einer Schulausgabe vorliegenden Farce Absurd Person Singular von von Alan Ayckbourn[36], kann ich doch an passenden Stellen diese oder jene Eigenschaft der Farce als solche an Black Comedy herausstellen. Am Ende der Probenarbeit kann eine Zusammenfassung dieser Elemente für einen von den Schülern zu erstellenden Programmheftartikel als Grundlage dienen. Eine ausdrückliche Behandlung des Themas "Farce" als Bestandteil der Arbeit der Theater-AG halte ich nicht für günstig, da das als zu unterrichtsmäßig empfunden werden und dadurch motivationsmindernd wirken könnte.

Im einzelnen sind folgende Eigenschaften einer Farce zu nennen:

a) Wie in den meisten Farcen überwiegt auch in Black Comedy die Situationskomik gegenüber der Dialogkomik.

b) "Paradoxically, the crudest of all comic forms is a demanding, even a challenging style for dramatist and actor alike."[37]

c) Farce ist eine mechanische Form des Komischen: sowohl die Handlung als auch die Figuren werden nach mechanischen Gesetzmäßigkeiten manipuliert. Darin unterscheiden sich Farcen von flexibleren Formen dramatischer Komik.[38]

d) Das Prinzip der Komik ist in der Farce Black Comedy ein kindisches Vergnügen des Zuschauers am Unglück der Hauptfigur.

e) Alle Figuren in Black Comedy werden letztendlich durch höhere Gewalt, durch "a cosmic practical joke"[39] in die komischen Situationen gebracht: Die Dunkelheit, die die Abfolge der komischen Situationen einleitet, ist sowohl ungewollt als auch unverschuldet, und damit höhere Gewalt.

f) <u>B</u>lack <u>C</u>omedy ist nach dem Schneeball-Prinzip strukturiert. Das Unheil beginnt recht gemäßigt und nimmt mit der Zeit immer mehr zu, bis am Ende nichts mehr so ist, wie es am Anfang war.[40]

g) Farce ist beim Publikum sehr beliebt, in der Literaturkritik wird sie jedoch vernachlässigt.

5. Wissen über Sender und Adressaten

In ihrer Arbeit in der Theater-AG können die Schüler erkennen, daß die Sprache und die Sprechweise auf der Bühne anders sein müssen als im täglichen Leben:

Learning to act emphasizes the importance of voice control, projection, pitch and articulation, and creates an awareness of the non-verbal elements of communication, such as movement, gesture, facial expressions, pauses and silences.[41]

Hinzu kommt, daß die Schüler auch die Faktoren kennenlernen, die das professionelle Theater ausmachen: Funktionen von Schauspielern, Regisseur, Bühnenbild, Requisiten und Text in ihren jeweiligen Wechselbeziehungen. In einem fortgeschrittenen Probenstadium, wenn erstmals Mitschüler als Publikum hinzugebeten werden, erfahren die Schüler etwas über das mögliche Reaktionsverhalten auf bestimmte Situationen im Stück und lernen, auf Lacher oder Szenenapplaus richtig zu reagieren: weder zu früh noch zu spät weiterzumachen, denn im ersten Fall glaubt das Publikum bald, es dürfe nicht lachen (und das soll es ja bei einer Farce wie <u>B</u>lack <u>C</u>omedy), im zweiten Fall fällt die Spannung zu sehr ab.

6. Methodenbeherrschung

Im Bereich der Textrezeption ist als Methode die statarische
Lektüre als Voraussetzung für den Transfer des Textes auf die
Bühne zu nennen. Da der Text als Vorlage für eine Schülerauffüh-
rung in erster Linie von der Sprachverwendung her erschlossen
wird, "kommen Gestaltungsmittel der folgenden Ebenen in den
Blick (...): Lautebene, Wortebene, Satzebene und Textebene."[42]
Im Gegensatz zu der in den Richtlinien angebotenen Spezifizierung,
die sich auf die Interpretation von Texten bezieht, wird im Falle
der Einstudierung eines englischen Dramas der Umsetzungsprozeß
auf der Bühne im Vordergrund stehen. Auf der Lautebene wird es
somit weniger um rhetorische Figuren wie Alliterationen oder
Assonanzen gehen (zumindest nicht bei der Einstudierung von
Black Comedy), sondern allgemeiner um Aussprache und Intonation.
Auf der Wortebene werden die Schüler erkennen, daß die Figuren
durch Verwendung bestimmter Worte gezeichnet sind (Carol Melkett
durch das erwähnte "pegs"-Suffix und durch die Phrase "is
laughingly known as"). Auf den Englischunterricht bezogen stellt
Löffler fest:

Die fachspezifischen Möglichkeiten (des darstellenden Spiels)
liegen vorwiegend im Bereich der rezeptiven Kommunikations-
fähigkeit. Die Abfolge von Identifizieren über Diskriminieren
und Dekodieren zum sinnentnehmenden Verstehen des Laut- und/
oder Schriftbildes ist nicht weniger wichtig als die produkti-
ven Fertigkeiten, denen sie vorgeschaltet sind.[43]

Diese Aussage macht den Zusammenhang von Textproduktion und
Textrezeption deutlich. Die in den Bereich der Methodenbeherrschung
fallenden Verfahren und Teiloperationen der Texterschließung,
die oben aufgeführt wurden, erfolgen bereits alle mit Hinblick
auf die Textproduktion. Letztere findet zum einen in Form der gemeinsamen Auseinandersetzung um die Inszenierung statt: Vorschlä-
ge, die von den Schülern gemacht werden, müssen von ihnen auch
begründet werden können - ein methodischer Schritt der Argumentation.[44] Zum anderen erfolgt die Textproduktion in Form der Dar-

stellung von Rollen und Stückinhalt auf der Bühne. Dabei werden
Methoden eingeübt, gezielt Formen von Sprache einzusetzen, auf
die die Textrezeption schon verwies, und die sich auf Laut-, Wort-
und Satzebene finden. Doch neben die Methoden, die sich auf die
sprachliche Umsetzung der Dramentexte in eine Theateraufführung
beziehen, treten solche Methoden, die über die Sprache hinaus-
gehen und den ganzen Menschen, Intellekt, Emotionen, Mimik,
Gestik, Bewegungen, Gänge und den Einsatz der damit verbundenen
Mittel sowie die Interdependenz dieser Elemente betreffen.

In den Bereich der Methodenbeherrschung fallen schließlich
das Auswendiglernen des Textes und die Fähigkeit, vor einem
großen Publikum zu sprechen und zu spielen. Die spezifischen
Lernstrategien sind von Mensch zu Mensch verschieden. Jeder
Schüler wird im Laufe der Probenarbeit eigene Methoden entwickeln
müssen, den Text zu lernen und Lampenfieber nicht überhand nehmen zu lassen. Manche Schüler werden beim Textlernen mit einem
Cassettenrecorder arbeiten, andere brauchen eher visuelle Eindrücke, wieder andere beides, und je sicherer die Schüler den
Text beherrschen, desto leichter können sie wahrscheinlich ihr
Lampenfieber kontrollieren.

7. Haltungen und Einstellungen - die Verbindung von
   Theaterarbeit und Spracherwerb

Nicht nur fachspezifisch kann der Schüler durch die Einstudierung eines englischen Dramas wie Black Comedy im Rahmen einer
Theater-AG profitieren, sondern auch im Lernbereich Haltungen
und Einstellungen, einem Bereich, der dem allgemeinen Lernziel
der gymnasialen Oberstufe, Selbstverwirklichung in sozialer Ver-
antwortung, entspricht. 45)

Während zur Analyse der übrigen Lernbereiche die eher lern-
theoretisch ausgerichteten, neueren spieldidaktischen Ansätze er-
giebiger waren, ist es im Lernbereich Haltungen und Einstellungen

sinnvoll, auch auf die musisch-ästhetisch akzentuierende Richtung
einzugehen. So formulierte Amtmann: " Im darstellenden Spiel
wird der Mensch in seinem Denken, Fühlen und Handeln, in seiner
Gebundenheit von Seele, Geist und Körper, ins Spiel gebracht."[46]
Derart ganzheitlich verstanden vermittelt darstellendes Spiel
durch die Sinne eine Welterfahrung, die der Befähigung,"der Welt
in der Vielfalt der Erscheinungsformen geistig zu begegnen",
vorausgeht.[47] Die Ganzheitlichkeit des darstellenden Spiels be-
dingt, so Amtmann, weiterhin bleibendere Eindrücke und tieferge-
hende Wirkungen als ein nur mit dem Verstand vollzogener Unterricht.[48]

Die neuere Forschung akzentuiert mit ihrer Berufung auf die so-
ziologische Rollentheorie anders:

Darstellendes Spiel stellt für sozial-psychologisches Ver-
haltenstraining ein einmalig praxisbezogenes Übungsfeld bereit. Es ist in seiner Bedeutung für die verantwortliche
Vorbereitung des jungen Menschen auf die Rollenerfordernisse
der modernen Gesellschaft überhaupt nicht zu überschätzen.[49]

Diese und andere Aussagen über den sozio-psychologischen Wert des
darstellenden Spiels beziehen sich in erster Linie auf Rollenspiel, das den Nachvollzug von Alltagssituationen im Stegreifspiel und weniger die Umsetzung einer literarischen Vorlage vor
Publikum im Auge hat. Doch die positive Funktion eines derart
verstandenen darstellenden Spiels läßt sich auf die hier zu analy-
sierende Arbeit einer Theater-AG übertragen:

In der Theater-AG arbeiten die Schüler selbst- und mitverant-
wortlich in einer Gruppe auf ein gemeinsames Ziel hin: die Aufführung eines Dramas, die erfolgreich sein soll. Bei der Auswahl
der Rollen, besonders der Hauptrollen, aus der Betonung der eigenen Leistung einzelner Schüler, aus der Versuchung, Mitschüler
an die Wand zu spielen, können sich Probleme ergeben.[50] Ihre ge-
meinsame Lösung könnte Modellcharakter für andere, ähnliche Situationen innerhalb wie außerhalb des schulischen Rahmens haben.

Zu den positiven Wirkungen der Ganzheitlichkeit des Theaterspielens und der sozio-psychologischen Dimension, die nur kurz
angerissen wurden, treten noch einige weitere Faktoren, die
Stern so zusammenfaßt:

Drama encourages the operation of certain psychological
factors in the participant which facilitate self-esteem;
motivation; spontaneity; increased capacity for empathy;
and lowered sensitivity to rejection.[51]

Diese Faktoren sind im Bereich von Haltungen und Einstellungen
wichtig. Aber auch für den Spracherwerb Englisch spielen sie eine
große Rolle. Die folgenden Ausführungen stellen also die Verbindung von Haltungen und Einstellungen zum Spracherwerb Englisch
her!

Selbst-Wertschätzung, Motivation, Spontaneität, erhöhte
Empathiefähigkeit und geringere Empfindlichkeit gegenüber Ableh-
nung können unter dem Konzept des affektiven Filters zusammenge-
faßt werden. Dulay und Burt, die sich auf Krashens Monitor-
Theorie des Zweitsprachenerwerbs stützen und seine Terminologie
verwenden, formulieren diese Zusammenhänge so:

Faktoren der Einstellung

- ermutigen zur Aufnahme von Sprachmaterial
- befähigen den Lerner, das gehörte Sprachmaterial aktiv
  zu verwenden:
Simply hearing a second language with understanding appears
to be necessary but not sufficient for acquisition to take
place. The acquirer must not only understand the input but
must also, in a sense, be open to ist.[52]

Die Autoren sprechen vom socio-affective filter. Elemente dieses
Filters sind die bei Stern aufgezählten Faktoren. Am Beispiel
der Empathie läßt sich die Wirkung dieses Filters auf den Spracherwerb und die wichtige Rolle, die hierbei dem darstellenden
Spiel zukommen kann, besonders anschaulich verdeutlichen.

Die Fähigkeit des Einfühlungsvermögens hängt ab von der Fähigkeit "to partially and temporarily suspend the functions that
maintain one's separateness from others (usually called ego-
boundaries)".[53] Der Akt der Empathie ist ein zeitweises Aufgeben
der Ego-Begrenzungen zugunsten einer sofortigen, präkognitiven
Erfahrung des emotionalen Zustandes eines anderen Menschen als
des eigenen.[54] Die Fähigkeit nun, seine Aussprache so weit wie
möglich an die eines Sprechers der Zielsprache anzugleichen,
hängt ebenfalls mit der Flexibilität oder Durchlässigkeit der
Ego-Begrenzungen zusammen: Je höher die Empathie, je höher also
die Flexibilität oder Durchlässigkeit der Ego-Begrenzungen (d.h.
je niedriger der sozio-affektive Filter), desto besser ist die
Fähigkeit, sich der Zielsprache in der Aussprache möglichst weit
anzunähern. Schauspieler müssen große Empathie, d.h. große Ego-
Durchlässigkeit erreichen, um eine überzeugende Leistung zu
bringen.[55] Auch Schüler, die auf der Bühne stehen, werden also
durch den Versuch, echt zu wirken, Empathie entwickeln. Die damit verbundene höhere Durchlässigkeit der Ego-Begrenzungen wird
eine Sprachproduktion bewirken, die der Zielsprache näher kommt,
als es bei geringerer Durchlässigkeit der Ego-Begrenzungen, also
höherem affektiven Filter, der Fall wäre (etwa im Englischunterricht). In ähnlicher Weise dürften die anderen genannten Faktoren,
die den sozio-affektiven Filter ausmachen, im Bereich der Sprachbeherrschung und des Spracherwerbs wirksam sein.

Diese Ausführungen machen deutlich, daß nicht nur

a) die Umsetzung des englischen Dramas auf der Bühne und
b) die angestrebte englischsprachige Probenarbeit

den Spracherwerb Englisch fördern, sondern daß auch solche Elemente, die zunächst als recht getrennt vom Spracherwerbsprozeß
erscheinen mögen, nämlich nicht direkt sprachliche Aspekte der
Theaterarbeit, durchaus eine wichtige Rolle beim Spracherwerb
spielen. Die Verbindung von Haltungen und Einstellungen und
Spracherwerb Englisch ist damit hergestellt. Aus ihr ergibt sich

die Notwendigkeit, auch im Praxisbericht der Einstudierung
von Black Comedy auf diese Aspekte einzugehen.

Ein letzter Aspekt, der in den Bereich von Haltungen und Einstellungen fällt, besteht darin, daß die Schüler durch die Über-
nahme und Einübung von Methoden und Verfahren des professionel-
len Theaters in der Theater-AG viel über das Theater lernen. Die
dabei durch praktische Erfahrung gewonnenen Einsichten ermöglichen eine intensive theoretische Beschäftigung mit dem Theater
als Kunstform, sowie einen sicheren Umgang mit diesem Medium im
Sinne einer Theaterpädagogik, wie sie etwa von Beimdick vorgestellt wird.[56)]

8. Auswirkungen im Bereich des Englischunterrichts

Viele der bisher herausgearbeiteten Elemente der englischen
Theater-AG haben ihre Auswirkungen auf den Englischunterricht.
Auf der sprachlichen Ebene vertiefen die Schüler das im Englischunterricht Gelernte dadurch, daß sie es in den beiden Sprechsituationen der englischsprachigen Probenarbeit und in ihren Rollen in Black Comedy auf der Bühne anwenden müssen. Neues Sprech-
material kann im Sinne der Monitor-Theorie von Krashen erworben
und aufgrund des niedrigen sozio-affektiven Filters ebenfalls um-
gehend aktiv eingesetzt werden. Folglich ist anzunehmen, daß Mitglieder der Theater-AG sich im Unterricht besser ausdrücken können werden, die Aussprache wird klarer und zielsprachenangemes-
sener sein, und es wird ihnen zuhause, im Unterricht und bei
Klausuren leichter fallen, Texte sinnentnehmend zu lesen, da sie
intensives Lesen in der Theater-AG geübt haben.

Es handelt sich hier um begründete Möglichkeiten. Sie weisen
bereits auf ein Problem hin, das im letzten Abschnitt dieser
theoretisch-didaktischen Überlegungen behandelt wird:

9. Lernerfolgskontrolle

Es geht dabei um die Frage: Wie soll überprüft werden, welche
der Lernziele, die die theoretisch-didaktischen Überlegungen
nahelegen, der Schüler konkret und in welchem Ausmaß erreicht
hat. Relativ einfach läßt sich feststellen, ob der Schüler den
Text gelernt hat, ob er sinnvermittelnd spricht und dabei die
Mittel von Aussprache und Intonation adäquat einsetzt. Auch Mimik,
Gestik, Bewegungen und Gänge, die vorher festgelegt waren, lassen sich überprüfen. In anderen Fällen jedoch kann nicht eindeutig geklärt werden, welche Wirkungen auf den Englischunterricht
zurückzuführen sind und welche auf die Arbeit in der englischen
Theater-AG. Eher intuitive Feststellungen oder solche auf der
Grundlage wenig systematischer Beobachtungen, wie sie zum Beispiel Pflüger nach Schüleraufführungen französischer Klassiker
gibt[57], können leicht zu "typischen Fehlerquellen beim Lehrer-
urteil"[58] führen (zum Beispiel Halo-Effekt). Gefragt wären also
genaue Kriterien des zu beobachtenden (Sprach-) Verhaltens und
der Beobachtungsweisen sowohl in den jeweiligen Englischkursen
der Schüler als auch in der Theater-AG. Ein solches Projekt,wenn
es sprachwissenschaftlich-methodisch überhaupt zu realisieren
ist, übersteigt den Rahmen dieser Arbeit.

III. P R A X I S B E R I C H T

EINSTUDIERUNG VON BLACK COMEDY

1. Lern- und Lehrvoraussetzungen

Der vorliegende Praxisbericht beschäftigt sich mit der Einstudierung von Peter Shaffers Black Comedy in einer Theater-Arbeitsgemeinschaft, die sich aus neun Schülerinnen und einem Schüler der Jahrgangsstufen 11 - 13 des Ricarda-Huch-Gymnasiums,
Krefeld, zusammensetzte. Probenbeginn war am 9. 10. 1986, Premiere am 12.03.1987. Im Gegensatz zu benoteter Arbeit im Rahmen
eines Literatur-Grundkurses handelt es sich bei der Form der
Theater-AG um eine unbenotete, außerunterrichtliche Schulveran-
staltung. Alle Schüler nehmen aus Interesse an dieser AG teil.
Wahlpflichtüberlegungen zur Absicherung der drei in den Richtlinien Nordrhein-Westfalens festgelegten Aufgabenfelder (hier:
Feld (1), sprachlich-literarisch-künstlerischer Bereich[59]) sind
nicht gegeben. Die Motivation der Teilnehmer ist dadurch zunächst
allgemein sehr hoch zu veranschlagen; Das Lehrer-Schüler-Verhält-
nis wird aufgelockert, und die Ziele der Theater-AG werden leichter erreichbar sein. Vier Schülerinnen haben zudem im vorausge-
gangenen Schulhalbjahr bereits an dieser englischen Theater-AG
teilgenommen und in Alan Ayckbourns Einakter A Talk in the Park
und Mother Figure auf der (Schul-)Bühne nicht nur am Ricarda-Huch-
Gymnasium in Krefeld, sondern für eine Gastvorstellung auch am
Theodor-Schwann-Gymnasium in Neuss gespielt. Ein weiterer Aspekt
mit motivierender Wirkung ist, daß in dieser Theater-AG Stücke
von englischen Dramatikern in englischer Sprache aufgeführt werden. Auch die Erarbeitung des Dramas auf den Proben soll in englischer Sprache erfolgen. Der Reiz des Neuen, der von etwas so
selten Praktiziertem ausgeht, darf nicht unterschätzt werden. Dem
Aspekt des Theaterspielens, der an sich schon für viele Schüler
anregend ist, gesellt sich also noch der der Fremdsprachigkeit
als motivationssteigernd hinzu. Zwei Schülerinnen der Jahrgangs-

stufe 13 wollen nach dem Abitur Schauspielerin beziehungsweise
Regisseurin werden und nehmen das Angebot der Theater-AG als prak-
tisches Erprobungsfeld für den angestrebten Beruf wahr. Sie werden sich vermutlich auch besonders engagieren, ebenso wie die
zwei Schülerinnen der Jahrgangsstufe 12, die jeweils ein Jahr in
den USA beziehungsweise in Australien waren. Ihre,,den anderen
Teilnehmern der Theater-AG überlegenen,sprachlichen Fertigkeiten
werden sicherlich für sie selbst, aber auch für die übrigen Mitglieder der AG fruchtbar sein: da es sich um bei den anderen an-
erkannte, ihre Vorzüge nicht zur Schau stellende Schülerinnen
handelt, sehe ich die Gefahr, daß Eifersucht oder Überreaktionen
auf Verbesserungen durch diese beiden Schülerinnen aufkommen, als
sehr gering an. Verbesserungen der Intonatioon und der Aussprache
können vielmehr auf die Schüler delegiert werden. Darüberhinaus
erwarte ich, daß die Schülerinnen, die ein Jahr im englischsprachigen Ausland fast ausschließlich auf Kommunikation in englischer Sprache angewiesen waren, auf die Probensprache Englisch
eher eingehen werden als die anderen Schüler, die das meiner Erfahrung aus dem vergangenen Schulhalbjahr nach nur zögernd tun.
Die anderen Schüler könnten dann diesem Beispiel folgen.

Von den zehn teilnehmenden Schülern haben acht Englisch als
sechsstündigen Leistungskurs gewählt, eine Schülerin ist in der
Jahrgangsstufe 11.1, in der noch keine Differenzierung zwischen
Grundkurs und Leistungskurs erfolgt ist, sie will jedoch Englisch
mit Beginn der 11.2 ebenfalls als Leistungskurs wählen. Eine
Schülerin der 12.1 hat Englisch im Grundkurs, sie war jedoch ein
Jahr in Australien. Alle Schüler bringen damit zum einen gute
Voraussetzungen für die englische Theater-AG mit. Zum anderen
wird sich für sie die intensive Auseinandersetzung mit der eng-
lischen Sprache in der Theater-AG positiv auf den Englischunterricht auswirken.

Als Bedingungsfaktoren für die Theaterarbeit sind auch allgemeine künstlerische Begabungen zu nennen. Mehrere Schüler haben
einen Kunst-Leistungskurs gewählt, oder sie wirken aktiv im
Schulchor oder Schulorchester mit. Dies wird sich beim kreativen

Erfassen und Gestalten der Rollen günstig auswirken, denn solche
Schüler kennen bereits das kreative Gestalten von vorliegendem
Material in Form der Musikpartitur. Dramentext und Partitur sind
nicht Selbstzwecke; sie sind vielmehr die Vorlagen, die zusammen
mit der Interpretation durch darstellendes Spiel,beziehungsweise
durch Instrumente und Stimme,den ganzheitlichen Charakter der
Kunstwerke Drama und Musik ausmachen. Nicht nur die Umsetzung ist
diesen Schülern vertraut, sondern auch die zumindest in Ansätzen
in der Schule zu realisierende künstlerische Arbeitsatmosphäre
des gemeinsamen Schaffens, die sich im Laufe der Proben entwickelt
und als sehr förderlich für die Arbeit angesehen werden muß.

Da meine Mutter Schauspielerin ist, bin ich gewissermaßen mit
dem Theater groß geworden. Mit sechs Jahren stand ich in einer
Version von Aschenputtel erstmals selbst auf der Bühne (Staats-
theater Oldenburg). 1971 spielte ich am Rheinischen Landestheater
den Jungen in Beckets Warten auf Godot. In der Theater-AG des
Theodor-Schwann-Gymnasiums in Neuss habe ich dreimal mitgewirkt:
Als Junker Andreas in Was Ihr Wollt, als Bazillus in Turrinis
Der Tollste Tag und als Erscheinung des Dareios in Aischylos,
Die Perser.

Folglich habe ich sowohl direkte und indirekte Erfahrung mit
professionellem Theater als auch mit der Arbeit in einer Theater-
AG. Von September 1979 bis August 1980 arbeitete ich als Assistant
Teacher in der Nähe von London; dort nutzte ich meine Freizeit
zu zahlreichen Theaterbesuchen und arbeitete mich besonders in
das zeitgenössische englische Drama ein. In den Semesterferien
der kommenden Jahre folgten weitere London-Aufenthalte. Für meine
Dissertation über Künstlerbiographien im Zeitgenössischen Englischen Drama, an der ich zur Zeit bei Prof. Dr. Albert-Reiner
Glaap, Universität Düsseldorf arbeite, erhielt ich ein viermona-
tiges Promotionsstipendium vom DAAD, durch das ich meine Theater-
Erfahrung noch vertiefen konnte.

2. Planung

Die zeitliche Planung mit den dazugehörigen Inhalten geht aus der umseitigen Übersicht hervor. Ich hatte die Proben vom 09.10. 1986 - 18.12.1986 genauer geplant als die vom 8.1. - 12.3. 1987; einmal, weil die Planung eine Teilaufgabe der Zweiten Staatsexamensarbeit darstellte, die diesem Buch zugrundeliegt. Zum anderen erfordern gerade die Proben von längeren Stückabschnitten eine flexiblere Probenplanung, je nach den organisatorischen Gegebenheiten. Um kleine, überschaubare Einheiten probieren zu können, habe ich Black Comedy in zehn Szenen eingeteilt. Das Kriterium war dabei das Auftreten beziehungsweise Abgehen der Figuren (mit Ausnahme von Brindsley). Vor der Probe lesen die Schüler die anstehende(n) Szene(n) jeweils laut zuhause und lernen, wenn möglich, schon den Text. Szenen mit wenigen vorgegebenen Regieanweisungen lasse ich zunächst von den Schülern auf der Bühne vorspielen. Falsch ausgesprochene Worte werden von den Mitschülern oder von mir korrigiert. Dabei überlege ich mir von Fall zu Fall (personen- und situationsabhängig), ob ich den Fehler sofort, im Redefluß des Schülers, verbessere, oder ob ich dem Schüler erst einmal die Möglichkeit gebe, eine Passage zuende zu sprechen, um dann Schritt für Schritt die Verbesserungen vorzunehmen. Im zweiten Durchgang achten wir auf Gänge, Bewegungen, Gestik und Mimik; zum Teil ergeben sich aus den Verbesserungsvorschlägen dazu bereits Intonationsveränderungen, die sonst im dritten Durchgang besonders berücksichtigt werden. In den weiteren Durchgängen, auch auf späteren Proben, entstehen Änderungsvorschläge entweder intuitiv aus der Probensituation oder als Folge der häuslichen Vorbereitung der Szenen. Sie können sich aber auch aus Unzufriedenheit mit irgendeinem Vorgang auf der Bühne ergeben.

Szenen, die eine größere Koordination von zum Teil zahlreichen Gängen mit den Dialogen erfordern, werden gleich von Anfang an von mir gestellt, um die Schüler weder zu überfordern noch zu sehr zu frustrieren. Ich empfehle den Schülern, Einzelheiten der Dialogregie (Pausen, Betonungen, gegebenenfalls auch die Aussprache der als schwer empfundenen Worte) und der Bewegungsregie schriftlich festzuhalten und mache mir selbst entsprechende Notizen im Regiebuch (Siehe Anhang). Wenn die einstudierte Szene in einer späteren Sitzung wieder aufgegriffen wird und noch verfeinert werden soll, wird sich zeigen, in welchem Ausmaß das Erarbeitete sich gesetzt, und ob der Schüler den Text adäquat gelernt hat.

Übersicht der Planung

Termin	Szene	
9.10.	1	
16.10.	2, 3	
23.10.	4	(Lese- und Sprechprobe)
6.11.	4	
13.11.	5	
20.11.	6	
27.11.	7	
4.12.	8, 9, 10	
11.12.	Stückprobe 1 - 10	
18.12.	Stückprobe 1 - 10	

3. Durchführung

a) Organisatorische Gegebenheiten

Wie der Fachunterricht unterliegt auch die Arbeit der außerunter-
richtlichen Theater-AG organisatorischen Gegebenheiten:

1) In der Gruppe einigten wir uns auf den Termin donnerstags
16.30 - 18.00 Uhr. Klausurvorbereitungen, Fahrstunden und
Führerscheinprüfungen brachten es mit sich, daß einige Schüler an einer Probe oder mehreren nicht teilnehmen konnten.

2) Durch ein Mißverständnis mit dem Hausmeister war ich davon
ausgegangen, daß uns die Aula am 23.10.1986 nicht zur Verfügung stehen würde. Im Zeichensaal der Schule haben wir
dann gemeinsam die für das Bühnenbild benötigten "Gemälde"
hergestellt, wie sie auf Seite 185 in Black Comedy beschrie-
ben sind (Siehe auch Anhang, S.53). Im Anschluß daran fand
eine Sprechprobe der vierten Szene statt.

3) Am 4.12. 1986 wurden abends in der Schule die beiden Einakter
A Talk in the Park und Mother Figure von Ayckbourn wieder aufgeführt. Die Schülerinnen, die darin mitspielten, wollten ver-
ständlicherweise nicht vorher noch Black Comedy probieren,
zumal für 17.30 eine Wiederaufnahmeprobe für die beiden
Ayckbourn-Stücke angesetzt war. Ich habe an diesem Tag von
16.30 bis 17.30 mit den anderen Schülern eine Sprechprobe gemacht.

4) Die Konzentrations- und damit Arbeitsfähigkeit der Schüler
variierte von Probe zu Probe. Die Tagesform wurde besonders
durch Klausuren beeinträchtigt, die mehrfach donnerstags geschrieben wurden (für Schüler der Jahrgangsstufe 13 sechs-
stündig).

Diese Gegebenheiten führten dazu, daß der zeitliche Ablauf
nicht planmäßig verlief. Im Vergleich mit dem Plan kann der tat-
sächliche Probenverlauf der folgenden Übersicht entnommen werden.

b) Zeitlicher Probenverlauf

Termin	Probe
9.10.	Szene 1
16.10.	Szenen 2, 3
23.10.	Lese- und Sprechprobe Szene 4
	Arbeit am Bühnenbild
6.11.	Szene 4 (Stückprobe, erste Hälfte)
13.11.	Szene 4 (Stückprobe, zweite Hälfte)
20.11.	Szene 4 gesamt
27.11.	Szenen 5, 6, 7
4.12.	Sprechprobe mit den Schülern, die nicht in den Ayckbourn-Einaktern mitwirkten.
11.12.	Szenen 8, 9, 10
18.12.	Stückprobe Szenen 1 - 5
8. 1.	Szenen 6 - 10
15. 1.	Szene 4
22. 1.	Szene 4
29. 1.	Szenen 1 - 5
12. 2.	Szenen 1 - 5
19. 2.	Szenen 6 - 10
26. 2.	Szenen 6 - 10
5. 3.	Szene 4
9. 3.	ganz
12. 3.	ganz Premiere.

c) Besetzung der Rollen

Ich habe den Schülern die von Peter Shaffer in der Penguin-
Ausgabe von Black Comedy abgedruckte Beschreibung der Figuren
des Stückes vorgelesen und ihnen den Inhalt kurz auf Englisch
erzählt. Anschließend lasen die Schüler das Stück laut mit ver-
teilten Rollen vor; dabei tauschten sie hin und wieder nach
eigenen Wünschen und nach meinen Anregungen die Rollen, um dadurch verschiedene Figuren selbst kennenzulernen. Danach legten
wir gemeinsam die Besetzung fest. Ich habe mich dabei bewußt
zurückgehalten, um die Entscheidungen der Schüler nicht zu beein-
flussen. In einigen Fällen hat mich die Wahl der Schüler über-
rascht, weil ich die Rollen anders empfunden beziehungsweise die
Schüler anders eingeschätzt hatte. Ich entschloß mich jedoch,
auch diese Entscheidungen der Schüler zu akzeptieren, mit dem
Gedanken, auf den Proben das Beste daraus zu machen und gegebenenfalls die Schüler dahin zu führen, Grenzen ihrer Leistungsfähig-
keit zu erkennen, aber auch, nicht zu bescheiden zu sein. In der
Probenarbeit ergab sich, daß die Schülerinnen Ansätze brachten,
die ich nicht erwartet hatte, und die ich gut ausbauen konnte. Bei
Ulrike beispielsweise, die ich mir eher in der Rolle der Clea
vorgestellt hatte, erwies sich die sehr gute Aussprache (durch
einjährigen Australienaufenthalt) als beinahe unverzichtbare
Voraussetzung für die Gestaltung ihrer Rolle des Harold Gorringe.
Dadurch, daß sie sich beim Spielen nicht auf die Aussprache kon-
zentrieren mußte, konnte sie ihre Aufmerksamkeit auf die Nuancie-
rung der Intonation richten, um so Harold Gorringe als Homosexuellen zu charakterisieren. Ein weiteres Beispiel: Kirsten hatte in
Mother Figure die Titelrolle, Lucy, gespielt. Durch diesen Ein-
druck voreingenommen, hatte ich sie ursprünglich nicht unbedingt
in der Rolle der Clea, die sie sich in Black Comedy ausgewählt
hatte, gesehen. In der Tat hatte sie zunächst Schwierigkeiten,
den Tonfall der Lucy abzulegen, besonders nach der Wiederaufnahme
der Ayckbourn-Einakter im Dezember. Doch sehr bald, nachdem ich
ihr dieses Problem klargemacht hatte, arbeitete sie erfolgreich
an der Intonation und wurde als Clea immer überzeugender, nicht
nur für mich, sondern auch für die Mitspieler.

d) Doppelbesetzungen

Erstmals entschloß ich mich in dieser Theater-AG dazu, mit Doppelbesetzungen zu arbeiten. Dies hatte folgende Gründe: Einmal wollten zehn Schüler an der Theater-AG teilnehmen, zwei mehr, als Rollen in Black Comedy zur Verfügung stehen. Ein zeitgenössisches englisches Drama mit zehn Personen, das für die Theater-AG interessant, kurz genug und nicht zu anspruchsvoll ist, habe ich nicht gefunden. Im zeitgenössischen englischen Drama ist die Zahl der Zwei- bis Vierpersonenstücke weitaus größer. Zum anderen habe ich an die besonderen Belastungen gedacht, die die Schüler der Jahrgangsstufe 13 mit ihren langen Klausuren und der Abiturvorbereitung haben. Die Gefahr, daß die Schüler aus Zeitgründen abspringen, ist dadurch größer als bei Schülern der Jahrgangsstufen 11 und 12.

Die Rolle der Miss Furnival wurde von einer Schülerin aus der 12 (Elke), die neu in der Theater-AG war, übernommen, und in zweiter Besetzung von einer Schülerin aus der 13 (Nadja), die bereits in Mother Figure mitgespielt hatte.Die Szenen, in denen Miss Furnival auftritt, habe ich meist mit Elke einstudiert, und Nadja konnte die relativ einfache Rolle entsprechend übernehmen. An einigen Stellen brachte sie spontan Neuerungen an, die Elke nach Diskussionen in der Gruppe zum Teil übernommen hat. Für Nadja, die auch im Schulorchester mitwirkt, war die Doppelbesetzung eine willkommene zeitliche Erleichterung. Es war ursprünglich geplant, daß die Schülerin, die jeweils in einer Aufführung von Black Comedy nicht spielt, die in diesem Stück sehr wichtige Aufgabe der Beleuchtung übernimmt.

Ulrike, die schon in A Talk in the Park Bühnenerfahrung hatte, spielte Harold Gorringe. Ursprünglich wollte (und sollte) auch Tatjana diese Rolle spielen, sie mußte jedoch die Mitarbeit in der Theater-AG relativ früh aus gesundheitlichen Gründen aufgeben. Auch in diesem Fall hat sich die anfängliche Doppelbesetzung bezahlt gemacht.

Isabel und Anke, beide neu in der Theater-AG, einigten sich
darauf, Schuppanzigh und Bamberger, zwei recht kleine Rollen,
abwechselnd zu spielen und ansonsten die Aufgabe des Soufflierens zu übernehmen.

e) Englisch als Probensprache

Die Schüler bestanden darauf, daß ich meine Bemerkungen, Kom-
mentare und Regieanweisungen in englischer Sprache gab und er-
mahnten mich, wenn ich "versehentlich" Deutsch sprach. Sie selbst
jedoch ließen sich nur sehr schwer dazu bewegen, auch Englisch
zu sprechen. Wenn sie es taten, dann mit einer hohen Korrektheit
und einer Ausdrucksfähigkeit, die die in dem von mir beobachte-
ten und selbst gehaltenen Englischunterricht dieser Schüler über-
schritt. Die Schüler, die schon in den Einaktern von Ayckbourn
mitgewirkt hatten, waren eher bereit, auf den Proben Englisch zu
sprechen, besonders, nachdem sie die Stücke erfolgreich wieder
aufgeführt hatten. Erwartungsgemäß zeigte sich auch bei den beiden Schülerinnen mit Auslandsaufenthalt, daß sie öfter Englisch
sprachen als die anderen Mitglieder der Theater-AG; zumindest
anfänglich übertrug sich das hingegen nur wenig auf die anderen.

f) Dialogregie

Die Dialogregie konzentriert sich auf die drei Bereiche
Aussprache, Lautstärke und Intonation.

Aussprache

Die Sprache in Black Comedy ist alltägliches Englisch, das
Stück beinhaltet daher nur recht wenige Worte, die für die Schüler schwer auszusprechen waren. Am häufigsten zeigten sich Fehler bei der Silbenbetonung, beispielsweise beim Wort "antique".

Schwieriger war es, falsche Aussprache zu korrigieren, die die
Schüler sich über Jahre hinaus angewöhnt zu haben scheinen, etwa
w ri statt w ri (Hier fällt auch die unterschiedliche Aussprache
in England, den USA und Australien ins Gewicht).

Bezüglich der Deutlichkeit der Aussprache mußte ich besonders
darauf achten, daß die Schüler nicht undeutlich von einem Wort
zum anderen glitten, so daß letztlich nichts zu verstehen war.
Um zu erreichen, daß die Konsonanten deutlich zu hören waren,
durften die Schüler auf der Bühne nicht so schnell sprechen, wie
sie das möglicherweise vom Englischunterricht her gewöhnt waren.
Schwierigkeiten bereitete eine unmittelbare Aufeinanderfolge von
"s" und "th", etwa in "is there". In den Anfangsstadien sprachen
die Schüler oft in beiden Worten entweder nur "s" oder nur "th".
Ich bin auf solche Schwächen immer wieder eingegangen und habe
nicht locker gelassen, bis eine korrekte und deutliche Aussprache
erreicht war. Im Laufe der Zeit haben die Schüler selbst auf die
Aussprache der Mitschüler geachtet und sie, wenn notwendig, un-
abhängig von mir korrigiert.

In der Wiederaufführung der Ayckbourn-Einakter im Dezember
1986 haben die Schüler sich sehr viel mehr Zeit nicht nur mit
den Bewegungen, sondern auch mit dem Sprechen gelassen, mit
großem Erfolg. Diese direkte Erfahrung, die sicherlich noch durch
die Probenarbeit mit Black Comedy begünstigt wurde, hatte ihrer-
seits wiederum deutliche Auswirkungen auf die sprachliche Cha-
rakterisierung der Figuren in Black Comedy. Nicht nur die Schüler, die in A Talk in the Park und Mother Figure mitgespielt
hatten, sondern auch die anderen Mitglieder der Theater-AG er-
reichten dadurch eine wesentlich deutlichere Aussprache als zuvor.

Lautstärke

Sehr unterschiedlich ist die Fähigkeit der verschiedenen
Schüler, laut zu sprechen. Das liegt zum einen an den verschiedenen Stimmvolumina. Zum anderen haben die Schüler offenbar an-

fänglich kein Gefühl dafür, wie laut oder leise sie sprechen. Um
dies Gefühl zu vermitteln, unterhielt ich mich von der letzten
Reihe der Aula aus mit den Schülern, die auf der Bühne standen,
zunächst auf Deutsch, dann bald auf Englisch, über alltägliche
Dinge. Dabei versuchte ich, die Lautstärke und die Deutlichkeit
der Schüleräußerungen in meinen jeweiligen Antworten zu imitieren.
In einem zweiten Schritt ließ ich auf diese Weise den Text von
Black Comedy laut lesen oder auswendig sprechen und imitierte
undeutliche Aussprache, oder fragte einfach mitten im Satz:
"Pardon?", wenn ich die Worte der Schüler nicht laut genug ge-
hört hatte. Später setzte ich mich dann in die erste Reihe und
achtete darauf, daß die Schüler nicht wieder leiser wurden.

Sprechtechnik beruht unter anderem auf einem richtigen Einsatz des Zwerchfells. Um den Schülern ein Gefühl dafür zu vermitteln, empfahl ich ihnen, sich auf den Rücken zu legen,
schwere Bücher auf den Bauch zu packen und dann laut die Vokale
zu sagen. Dabei spannt sich das Zwerchfell automatisch an. Auf
der Bühne können die Schüler das Zwerchfell dann bewußt anspan-
nen und so eine Überanstrengung der Stimme vermeiden. Vielen
Schülern erschien eine solche Übung albern. Einige versuchten es
jedoch, und es half ihnen.

Intonation

Die Figuren in Black Comedy sind als Typen gezeichnet, und
gerade durch die Intonation läßt sich das sehr gut herausarbei-
ten. Im einzelnen verweise ich auf die entsprechenden Abschnitte
des ersten Kapitels.

Zum großen Teil hatten die Schüler diese Charakteristika der
Sprache bereits beim Lesen erfaßt. Meine Aufgabe bestand darin,
Nuancen herauszuarbeiten. Dazu einige Beispiele:
    Für eine Passage auf S. 189 (Anhang: Regiebuch, S. 7b)
    schlug ich vor, daß Carol ihre Fragen an Brindsley über Clea
    von "Tell me, Brin..." bis "Well, why did you still have her

photo in your bedroom drawer?" mit zunehmender Schnelligkeit
und Schärfe stellt, während Brin immer zögernder antwortet.

- Bei der zweiten Probe der ersten Szene sagte Silvia als
  Brindsley versehentlich: "And let my neighbour Harold
  Gorringe never find out that we stole (statt "borrowed")
  his furniture behind his back. Amen." (S. 189-190; Regiebuch
  S. 7-9). Diese Version behielten wir bei.

- Da wir weder den Text noch die Melodie von Rock the Ages
  in Erfahrung bringen konnten (dieses Lied muß Miss Furnival
  singen), entschieden wir uns, daß Miss Furnival stattdessen
  die erste Zeile der englischen Nationalhymne singt. Elke
  hatte Schwierigkeiten, auch außerhalb der Rolle, richtig zu
  singen; erst nach einiger Überredung durch die Gruppe sah
  sie ein, daß gerade ein unerschrocken falsches Singen für
  die Rolle an dieser Stelle sehr gut ist, denn Miss Furnival
  soll hier stockbetrunken sein.

- Besonders Harold Gorringe läßt sich dem Klischee der Sprech-
  weise eines Homosexuellen entsprechend durch Variation der
  Intonation charakterisieren. Im fortgeschrittenen Probensta-
  dium kamen dazu immer neue Anregungen von Ulrike und der
  Gruppe. Aus "Hello? Hello? Anyone there?" (S. 199; Anhang
  S. 17b) wurde: "Helloohhooo? Hellooohoooo? Aanyone theheere?",
  Harolds Worte über Brindsley, "He's a very sweet boy" (S.203;
  Anhang S. 21b) sprach Ulrike entsprechend besonders süßlich.

g) Bewegungsregie

Auch die Bewegungsregie werde ich in diesem Kapitel behandeln,
da hierbei sehr viele Regieanweisungen und entsprechende Diskussionen in englischer Sprache in der Theater-AG zum Tragen kamen,
die ebenso wie die Dialogregie dem Spracherwerb Englisch dienten.

Grundlegende Ebene der Bewegungen in Black Comedy

Die Situationskomik in **Black** **Comedy** besteht grundlegend darin, daß die Schauspieler mit offenen Augen so tun müssen, als sähen sie nichts, weil sie im Dunkeln sind. Das bedeutet, daß sie absichtlich gegen Mobiliar oder Mitspieler rennen müssen, ohne daß das Publikum diese Absicht als solche erkennt.

Bei ihren ersten Versuchen liefen die Schüler mit normal seitlich herabhängenden Armen und nur wenig verminderter Geschwindigkeit zielstrebig über die Bühne und verminderten ihr Tempo lange vor dem Hindernis, mit dem sie zusammenprallen sollten. Ich half daraufhin, mehrere Tische, Stühle und an diesem Tag zufällig in einer Ecke der Bühne stehende Blechfässer wahllos auf der Bühne zu verteilen. Dann wurde das Licht ausgeschaltet und die Schüler mußten mit geschlossenen Augen vorsichtig auf der Bühne umhergehen. Es war gerade noch so hell in der Aula, daß ich vom Zuschauerraum aus warnend eingreifen konnte, wenn ein Schüler zu nahe an die Rampe kam. Zuerst gingen die Schüler sehr selbstsicher los, bald jedoch hatten sie sich oft gestoßen oder sie waren mit Mitschülern zusammengeprallt. Dabei hatten sie sich immer sehr erschreckt. Sie begannen, langsamer zu gehen, mit ausgestreckten Armen tasteten sie sich vor und setzten einen Fuß vorsichtig vor den anderen. Nachdem alle Schüler dieses Stadium erreicht hatten, bat ich sie, nun nicht länger als Privatpersonen herumzulaufen, sondern in ihren Rollen. Die nächste Stufe bestand darin, daß die Schüler mit geschlossenen Augen bei Licht gehen mußten, dann bei Licht mit offenen Augen. Die Schüler kamen dabei selbst auf die Idee, daß der Blick im "Dunkeln" anders sein muß, als bei Licht: starr,ungerichtet. Im Verlauf der Probenzeit mußte ich zumindest die letzten Stufen dieses Bewegungstrainings mehrmals wiederholten.

Bewegungsabläufe

Die Bewegungsregie in Black Comedy bezieht sich nicht nur auf diese grundlegende Ebene. Ein Beispiel soll das verdeutlichen:

Als Colonel Melkett auftritt, macht er sein Feuerzeug an und geht neugierig durch den Raum. Während seines Gesprächs mit seiner Tochter Carol geht Miss Furnival sehr dicht im Gleichschritt hinter ihm her. Die Bemerkung des Colonels "Not to me!" ist Stichwort dafür, daß der Colonel sich plötzlich umdreht. Er sieht Miss Furnival dicht hinter sich stehen und reagiert zunächst erstaunt: Kopf und Oberkörper bewegen sich zurück. Das Erstaunen wird Empörung: er bewegt Kopf und Oberkörper in Miss Furnivals Richtung, sieht sie zornig an und drängt sie so immer weiter zurück, bis sie schließlich auf das Sofa plumpst. Bei diesem Bewegungsablauf fällt der Blick des Colonel auf Brindsleys Skulptur und er fragt: "What the hell's that?" (S.195; Anhang S. 13b).

Die Schüler neigten dazu, derartige Bewegungsabläufe, wenn sie erst einmal einstudiert waren, sehr schnell zu spielen und dann nur noch anzudeuten, weil sie ihnen geläufig waren. Ich erklärte ihnen dann die Notwendigkeit einer geradezu zeitlupenhaften Langsamkeit dieser Abläufe, damit das Publikum, das sie nicht kennt, sie nachvollziehen und dadurch darüber lachen kann.

Im Verlauf der Proben zeigte sich ferner, daß die Regieanweisungen im Text nicht durchgängig sind: häufig wird lediglich die für eine komische Situation notwendige Position (B) einer Figur angegeben, nicht aber, wann die Figur die vorige Position (A) verläßt, um die angestrebte Position (B) zu erreichen. Die im Text zu findenden Regieanweisungen mußte ich also zusammen mit den Schülern ergänzen und darüberhinaus mit den Gegebenheiten der Bühne am Ricarda-Huch-Gymnasium in Krefeld und denen des Dialogs koordinieren. Auch dazu ein Beispiel:

Die Passage auf S. 204 (Anhang S. 22b), "He reaches (...)
noiselessly" mußte in unserer Inszenierung geändert werden, da
keine für alle Zuschauer sichtbare Tür vorhanden ist. Brindley
wird also "im off" eine Tür zuwerfen und kurz darauf, auf das
Stichwort "drinks" (Carol),wieder erscheinen und sich die Positionen der drei Stühle in Erinnerung rufen, indem er mit dem
Zeigefinger auf sie zeigt. Auf das Stichwort "Daddy" (Carol)
geht er in Richtung Stuhl (1). Bei "bottles" (Carol) stößt er
mit Carol zusammen. Carols "It is very simple" kann Brindsley
auf sich beziehen, und er kommentiert das entsprechend mit einer
Grimasse.

Einige Dialoge zwischen Clea und Brindsley wurden in unserer
Aufführung gestrichen. Das hatte zwei Gründe: zum einen spielen
die Szenen in Brindsleys Schlafzimmer, das war bühnentechnisch
nicht realisierbar. Zum anderen wollten die beiden Schülerinnen,
die die Rollen von Clea und Brindsley verkörperten, keine Liebes-
szenen spielen.

h) Erste Durchlaufprobe am 18.12.1986

Für die letzte Probensitzung vor den Weihnachtsferien war ein
erster Durchlauf des gesamten Stückes geplant. Aus organisatorischen Gründen (abends fand in der Aula ein Schulkonzert statt,
für das auf 17.30 eine Probe angesetzt war) mußte unsere Probe
statt um 16.30 schon um 16.00 Uhr beginnen. Zwei Schülerinnen
hatten diese Terminverschiebung vergessen, so daß schon aus diesem Grunde nur die ersten fünf Szenen zu schaffen waren. Außer-
dem zeigte sich, daß die Schüler einige Regieanweisungen noch
nicht oder nicht eindeutig genug in ihrem Rollenbuch notiert und
sie deshalb vergessen hatten, so daß ich insbesondere in der sehr
langen und schwierigen vierten Szene immer wieder vom Zuschauerraum aus unterbrechen mußte. Darüberhinaus hatten viele Schüler
aus den Szenenzusammenhängen heraus neue, zum Teil sehr komische
Einfälle, über die die Mitspieler und ich dann immer herzlich

lachen mußten. Einige Schüler verfielen wieder der Angewohnheit,
zu schnell und damit zu undeutlich zu sprechen, vermutlich eine
Folge der Anspannung durch die Tatsache, daß erstmals mehrere
Szenen hintereinander probiert wurden. Besonders zeigte sich,
daß Silvia als Brindsley von Anfang an zu übertrieben das Hek-
tisch-Verzweifelte durch ihre Intonation ausdrückte; das wirkte
unecht und ähnelte zu sehr der Intonation, durch die Ulrike das
Homosexuelle in Harold Gorringe herausbrachte.

i) Textlernen

Die Schüler, die in den Ayckbourn-Einaktern mitgespielt hatten,
lernten ihren Text,je nach zeitlicher Möglichkeit, von Anfang an
meist im Voraus. Die anderen Schüler erkannten bald, daß es sinnvoller ist, wenn man nicht immer mit dem Textbuch in der Hand
probieren muß. Auf diese Weise erhielten auch die beiden Souf-
leusen Übung darin zu erkennen was eine Kunstpause, und was
ein "Hänger" war.

j) Zusätzliche motivationssteigernde Faktoren

Äußere Umstände der verschiedensten Art können für die Arbeit
in einer Theater-AG anregend sein. Ich möchte das an einigen
aktuellen Beispielen der Einstudierung von Black Comedy verdeutlichen.

Zeitungsrezension zu den Ayckbourn-Einaktern

Wenige Tage nach der Aufführung der Ayckbourn-Einakter erschien in der Rheinischen Post (Krefelder Stadtpost) eine nega-
tive, unqualifizierte Kritik, die die Schüler zunächst sehr er-
bost und auch entmutigt hat. Für die Schülerinnen, die nach dem
Abitur Regisseurin, Schauspielerin und freie Künstlerin (Malerin)

werden wollen und dann wirklich auch von unqualifizierten Presse-
kritikern abhängig sein können, war das eine Vorbereitung auf
die harte Berufspraxis, und die betreffenden Schülerinnen haben
das auch erkannt. Auf die Arbeit an Black Comedy war auch eine
Auswirkung dieser Kritik festzustellen: Während der zwei Proben,
die nach Erscheinen der Kritik vor den Weihnachtsferien statt-
fanden, war eine Steigerung der Intensität der Vorbereitung festzustellen, etwa nach dem Motto "Jetzt erst recht". Nach den Weihnachtsferien hatte sich diese Wirkung weitgehend verloren.

Hinzu kam jedoch, daß die Schüler einsahen, daß eine geziel-
tere Öffentlichkeitsarbeit notwendig ist, die sich nicht nur auf
die Billigung von Maßnahmen des Regisseurs beschränkt. Gemeinsam
beschlossen wir, DIN A3-Plakate zu entwerfen, die der Vater eines
Schülers fotokopieren konnte. Sie wurden rechtzeitig vor den Aufführungen von Black Comedy im März und Juli 1987 in Krefeld ver-
teilt. Auch die in Krefeld stationierte Britische Armee wurde
eingeladen.

Einzelproben

Es zeigte sich, daß auch die Ayckbourn-erfahrenen Schüler dazu
neigten, immer wieder zu schnell, zu undeutlich-undifferenziert
und zu leise zu sprechen. Um die Probenarbeit nicht ständig mit
diesen Grundlagen zu belasten und mehr Zeit für Nuancen zu haben,
machte ich besonders im klausurfreien Januar 1987 Einzelproben
mit den Schülern.

Bewerbung beim Schülertheater-Treffen Berlin

Ende November 1986 erhielt ich von der Leitung der Berliner
Festspiele GmbH auf Anfrage die Bewerbungsunterlagen für das 8.
Bundesweite Schülertheater-Treffen (8. - 16.06.1987). Sowohl die
Gruppe, die Black Comedy einstudierte, als auch die beiden Schü-
lerinnen, mit denen ich zu der Zeit Tom Kempinskis Duet for One

probierte, bewarben sich für dieses Treffen. Das war ein sehr
großer Anreiz für die Schüler, sich im Rahmen ihrer zeitlichen
Möglichkeiten noch intensiver mit ihren Rollen zu beschäftigen,
auch, weil bis zum 31.1.1987 eine Probe auf Video aufgezeichnet
und zusammen mit den übrigen Bewerbungsunterlagen bei der Fest-
spiel-GmbH eingereicht werden mußte. Am 30.01.87, dem Tag der
Zeugnisausgabe, haben wir das Videoband aufgenommen. Von 9.00
Uhr bis 15.00 Uhr waren die Schüler ohne nennenswerte Pause sehr
auf Präzision bedacht und voll konzentriert. Es war der erste
Gesamtdurchlauf des Stückes, oft mußten Szenen, vor allem auch
Szenenanschlüsse, wiederholt werden. Das Agieren vor der Kamera
und einigen zuschauenden Mitschülern brachte zunächst teilweise
Unsicherheit mit sich, die jedoch bald verschwand. Nach Beendi-
gung der immerhin sechsstündigen Arbeit waren die Schüler zwar
müde, aber doch angeregt; sie wußten, daß sie einiges geschafft
hatten. Ein Jurymitglied des Theatertreffens der Jugend sah sich
denn auch auf der Auswahlgrundlage des Videos die Premiere am
12.3. an.

k) Die Aufführungen am 12.03. und 09.07.1987

Nach den Weihnachtsferien ergab sich, daß Nadja kaum noch
Zeit hatte, zu den Proben zu kommen. Sie wollte aber wenigstens
das Soufflieren übernehmen, da Anke dabei von den Mitspielern
noch nicht so gut verstanden wurde. Am Tag der Premiere im März
wurde sie jedoch krank und Christiane, die in Ayckbourns A Talk
in the Park mitgewirkt hatte und gerade zwei Tage zuvor, am
10.3.,in dem "Rehearsed Reading" von Tom Kempinskis Duet for One
die Stephanie gespielt hatte, soufflierte in Black Comedy.
Wegen der Abiturvorbereitungen (Klausuren ab 26.3.1987) konnte
Kirsten (als Clea) sehr oft nicht zu den Proben kommen. So kam
es, daß erst am 12.3., in der Generalprobe am Tage der Premiere,
um 17.00 das Stück nach der einen Videoaufzeichnung erstmals ganz
im Zusammenhang gespielt werden konnte. Alle zeigten gute Nerven

und waren begeistert, daß die Generalprobe eine Katastrophe war,
denn dann mußte die Premiere ja ein Erfolg werden. So war es
denn auch. Unter der Anspannung übertrafen die Schüler sich
selbst, auch in der Meinung einiger Lehrer, die in Proben noch
stumm den Kopf geschüttelt hatten und nun begeistert waren. Vor
allem Elke war erst in der Generalprobe zu der unglaublichen
Komik gekommen, die dann auch in der Premiere zu mehrfachem
Szenenapplaus führte.

Im Juli 1987 wurde Black Comedy im Rahmen der Schülerkultur-
woche in Krefeld wieder aufgenommen. Anke soufflierte erfolgreich, weil Christiane die Rolle des Harold Gorringe übernehmen
sollte (Ulrike war schon in Ferien). Doch Christiane wurde zwei
Tage vor dem Termin krank, und Claudia, eine Schülerin der 12,
die vorher noch nie Theater gespielt hatte, übernahm kurzfristig
die Rolle (sie las ab). Auch diese Aufführung kam beim Publikum
sehr gut an.

4. Auswertung

Die ausgeführten Einzelaspekte der Probenarbeit an Black Comedy
führen zu folgenden Schlüssen:

a) Die organisatorischen Gegebenheiten sind unvermeidlich; sie
erfordern Flexibilität von den Darstellern und vom Regisseur.
Diese war in erfreulichem Umfang gegeben, so daß auf jeder
Probe Fortschritte erzielt wurden, auch wenn die Proben nicht
immer so abliefen, wie sie geplant waren.

b) Die Proben haben zweierlei bestätigt: einmal, daß meine Vor-
urteile bezüglich der Besetzungen der Rollen in den geschil-
derten Fällen unbegründet waren, und zum anderen, daß ich in
diesen Fällen mit dem Entschluß, den Schülern erst einmal
eine Chance zu geben, eine Rolle zu entwickeln, richtig lag.

c) Auch die Entscheidung, Doppelbesetzungen zuzulassen, erwies
sich als vorteilhaft: Im Falle von Nadja wurde die Belastung
zugunsten der Abiturvorbereitung abgeschwächt. Tatjanas ge-

sundheitsbedingtes Ausscheiden aus der Theater-AG war zwar be-
dauerlich, brachte aber keine Probleme für den weiteren Verlauf der Proben mit sich, da die Rolle des Harold Gorringe
auch mit Ulrike besetzt war, es also keinen Ausfall gab.
Schließlich war auch die Gefahr, daß Schüler, denen nur die
Aufgabe des Soufflierens bleibt, sich ungerecht behandelt
fühlen, nicht gegeben.

d) Als teilweise problematisch erwies sich Englisch als Probensprache. Hier spiegelt sich die Erfahrung wider, die sich
auf einer Fachkonferenz der Englischlehrer des Ricarda-Huch-
Gymnasiums, Krefeld, als die Erfahrung aller Englischlehrer
zeigte: Es fällt schwer, Schüler dazu zu bringen, sich außerhalb des Fachunterrichts Englisch in englischer Sprache zu
unterhalten, wenn kein "native speaker" dabei ist, der besten-
falls wirklich kaum Deutsch versteht.

Dennoch möchte ich an den theoretischen Begründungen fest-
halten, die ich im ersten Kapitel für Englisch als Probensprache angeführt habe. Die Tatsache, daß die Schüler darauf
bestanden haben, daß ich selbst Englisch sprach, führte dazu,
daß das Hörverstehen der Schüler gefördert werden konnte.
Vielleicht ist es möglich, die Hemmschwelle der Schüler dadurch zu senken, daß ich hin und wieder einen "native speaker"
zu den Proben bitte, dessen mangelnde Deutschkenntnisse es
erforderlich machen, daß die Schüler Englisch sprechen. Stures
Insistieren auf der englischen Sprache während der Proben
halte ich für wenig sinnvoll, da das entmotivierend wirken
würde.

e) Erst recht spät habe ich erkannt, daß die Regieanweisungen in
Black Comedy unvollständig sind. Es ist zwar gut, daß die
Schüler selbst auf die dadurch bedingten anfänglichen Unge-
reimtheiten hingewiesen haben, da es zeigte, wie gut sie das
Stück verstanden hatten. Aber die notwendigen Klarstellungen
waren recht zeitraubend und für die Schüler zum Teil verwir-
rend. Solche Unvollständigkeiten werde ich bei weiteren
Stücken schon vor Probenbeginn als möglich bedenken müssen,
um die Zeit der Proben sinnvoller nutzen zu können.

f) Es wäre sicherlich günstiger, wenn man in der Schul-Theater-AG mit der regelmäßigen Teilnahme der Schüler rechnen könnte. In der freiwilligen Theater-AG konnte ich - auch als Studienreferendar - die Schüler zwar begründet auffordern, regelmäßig zu kommen, zwingen konnte und wollte ich sie jedoch nicht. Das hätte den Spaß an der Sache zu sehr gefährdet. Und die Schüler haben auch selbst eingesehen, daß regelmäßigere Teilnahme besser gewesen wäre. Die englische Theater-AG in der Schule soll Spaß machen, nicht nur als Selbstzweck, sondern auch im Sinne einer Senkung des sozio-affektiven Filters zur Verbesserung des Spracherwerbs Englisch.

IV. ANMERKUNGEN

1) Hans Hoppe, "Theaterspielen als pädagogischer Erfahrungsraum", in: Handbuch der Spielpädagogik, Band 3. (Das Spiel als Erfahrungsraum und Medium). Herausgegeben von Karl Josef Kreuzer. (Düsseldorf, 1984), S. 316.

2) R. Newald, "Vom Späthumanismus zur Empfindsamkeit", in: H. de Boor und R. Newald, Geschichte der Deutschen Literatur, Band 5. (München ³1960), S. 94.

3) Hans Haven, Darstellendes Spiel. Funktionen und Formen. (Düsseldorf, 1970), S. 32.

4) Vgl. Hoppe, S. 317.

5) Vgl. ibid.,S. 318.

6) Gerhard Lippert, "Spieldidaktische Positionen heute", in: A.O. Schorb und Gertrud Simmerding (Hrsg.), Lehrerkolleg Spiel in der Schule. (München, 1980), S. 25.

7) Hoppe, S. 319.

8) Der Kultusminister des Landes Nordrhein-Westfalen, Richtlinien für die gymnasiale Oberstufe in Nordrhein-Westfalen: Englisch. (Köln, 1981), S. 7.

9) Vgl. Rudi Müller, "Darstellendes Spiel im Fachunterricht der gymnasialen Oberstufe", in: Herbert Giffei (Hrsg.), Theater machen - Ein Handbuch für die Amateur- und Schulbühne. (Ravensburg, 1982), S. 370-373.

10) Richtlinien Literaturkurse.

11) Norbert Kluge, Spielen und Erfahren. Der Zusammenhang von Spielerlebnis und Lernprozeß. (Bad Heilbrunn/Obb., 1981), S. 89.

12) Hoppe, S. 324.

13) Udo O.H.Jung, "Holistische Methoden fremdsprachlicher Unterweisung als Wegbereiter des neuen Schülertheaters. Eine Auswahlbibliographie", Die Neueren Sprachen 85:1 (1986), S. 57.

14) Peter Shaffer wurde 1926 in Liverpool geboren. Er studierte in Cambridge, arbeitete in einer Bibliothek in New York, bei einem Musikverlag in London, war von 1961-62 Musikkritiker der Zeitschrift Time and Tide und lebt heute als freier Schriftsteller in New York. 1957 wurden seine ersten beiden Dramen für das Fernsehen ausgestrahlt. 1958 erschien sein erstes Bühnenstück, Five Finger Exercise. 1962 kamen zwei Einakter (Komödien) heraus, The Public Eye und The Private Ear. 1964 wurde The Royal Hunt of the Sun am National Theatre ein großer Erfolg. 1965 lief am National Theatre die Farce Black Comedy. Mit White Liars (1968) und Shrivings (1970) war Shaffer nicht so erfolgreich, ganz im Gegensatz zu Equus (1973) und Amadeus (1979). Yonadab hatte im Dezember 1985 in London Premiere.

Im Anhang zu dieser Arbeit ist das Regiebuch der Einstudierung von Black Comedy abgedruckt. Der Text ist dem Buch The Collected Plays of Peter Shaffer (New York, 1982) entnommen.

15) Konrad Macht, Hilde Arnold, Gerda Geppert, Rita Hösl, Das darstellende Spiel im Englischunterricht. (Ansbach, 1977), S. 16.

16) Ibid.

17) Renate Löffler, Wulf-Michael Kunze, Spiele im Englischunterricht 2. (München, Wien, Baltimore, 1980), S. 24.

18) Paul Amtmann, "Spiel in der Schule - Zielsetzung und Verwirklichung", in: A.O. Schorb und Gertrud Simmerding (Hrsg.), Lehrerkolleg Spiel in der Schule. (München, 1980), S. 12.

19) Anne Frances Bulmer, "English through acting", Der Fremdsprachliche Unterricht 62 (1982), S. 147.

20) Vgl. The Collected Plays of Peter Shaffer. (New York, 1982), S. 183.

21) Vgl. Stephen Krashen, Second Language Acquisition and Second Language Learning. (Oxford, New York, Toronto, Sydney, Paris, Frankfurt, 1981), S. 2.

22) Vgl. Rod Ellis, "Informal and formal approaches to communicative language teaching", ELT Journal 36:2 (1982), S. 74.

23) Ibid., S. 75.

24) John Russell Taylor, Peter Shaffer. Writers and their Works Series. (Harlow, 1974), S. 22.

25) Henning Wode, Learning a Second Language. An Integrated View of Language Acquisition. (Tübingen, 1981), S. 59.

26) Vgl. Ellis, S. 80.

27) Vgl. ibid.

28) Ibid.

29) Bulmer, S. 146.

30) Richtlinien: Englisch, S. 30.

31) Ibid.

32) Peter Shaffer, Black Comedy, in: The Collected Plays of Peter Shaffer. (New York, 1982), S. 188; S. 194.

33) Ibid., S. 222 - 223.

34) Ibid., S. 198.

35) J.C. Trewin, Peter Brook, A Biography. (London, 1971), S. 92-93.

36) Vgl. Alan Ayckbourn, Absurd Person Singular . Herausgegeben von Albert Reiner Glaap. (Frankfurt, 19)

37) Jessica Milner Davis, Farce (Critical Idiom). (London, 1978), S. 17.

38) Vgl. ibid.,S. 23-24.

39) Ibid., S. 64.

40) Vgl. ibid.,S. 71.

41) Bulmer, S. 146.

42) Richtlinien: Englisch, S. 50-51.

43) Renate Löffler, Spiele im Englischunterricht. Vom lehrergelenkten Lernspiel zum schülerorientierten Rollenspiel. (München, Wien, Baltimore, 1979), S. 66.

44) Richtlinien: Englisch, S. 53.

45) Ibid., S. 16.

46) Paul Amtmann, "Darstellendes Spiel in der Schule", in: Paul Amtmann und Hermann Kaiser (Hrsg.), Darstellendes Spiel. Jugendspiel, Schulspiel, Volksspiel, Freilichtspiel, Studentenbühne, Amateurtheater. (Kassel und Basel, 1966), S. 26.

47) Ibid., S. 22.

48) Amtmann in "Spiel in der Schule", S. 11.

49) Erich Benedikt, Herbert Jungwirth und Walter Klaus (Hrsg.),
Schulspiel. Berichte über die gesamtösterreichische Arbeitstagung für
Lehrer an allgemeinbildenden höheren Schulen in Schloß Seggau bei
Leibnitz vom 28.5. - 1.6. 1971. (Wien, 1977), S. 17.

50) Vgl. B. Daublebsky, Spielen in der Schule.(Stuttgart, 1973), S. 162.

51) Susan L. Stern, "Drama in Second Language Learning from a Psycholinguistic Perspective", Language Learning 3:1 (1980), S. 77.

52) Krashen, S. 21.

53) Stern, S. 81.

54) Ibid.

55) Vgl. ibid.

56) Vgl. Walter Beimdick, Theater und Schule. Grundzüge einer Theaterpädagogik. (München, 1975).

57) Vgl. Helmut Pflüger, "Schüleraufführungen französischer Klassiker. Ein
Mittel zur Intensivierung französischen Sprachgefühls", Praxis des Neusprachlichen Unterrichts 13:2 (1966), S. 261-262.

58) Vgl. Hans-Peter Drögemüller, Handbuch für Studienreferendare.
(Stuttgart, 1977), S. 155f.

59) Richtlinien: Englisch, S. 22.

V. LITERATURVERZEICHNIS

Amtmann, Paul: "Darstellendes Spiel in der Schule". In: Amtmann, Paul und
Kaiser, Hermann (Hrsg.), Darstellendes Spiel. Jugendspiel, Schul-
spiel, Volksspiel, Freilichtspiel, Studentenbühne, Amateurtheater.
Kassel, Basel, 1966, S. 22-29.

Amtmann, Paul: "Spiel in der Schule - Zielsetzung und Verwirklichung".
In: A.O. Schorb, Gertrud Simmerding (Hrsg.), Lehrerkolleg Spiel
in der Schule. München, 1980, S. 7-17.

Ayckbourn, Alan: Confusions. Edited by Albert-Reiner Glaap.
Stuttgart, 1982.

Ayckbourn, Alan: Absurd Person Singular. Herausgegeben von Albert-Reiner
Glaap. Frankfurt, 19 .

Beimdick, Walter: Theater und Schule. Grundzüge einer Theaterpädagogik.
München, 1975.

Benedikt, Erich, Herbert Jungwirth, Walter Klaus (Hrsg.):
Schulspiel. Berichte über die gesamtösterreichische Arbeitstagung
für Lehrer an allgemeinbildenden höheren Schulen im Schloß Seggau
bei Leibnitz vom 28.Mai bis 1. Juni 1971. Wien, 1977.

Bulmer, Anne Frances: "English through Acting". Der Fremdsprachliche
Unterricht 62 (1982), S. 145-148.

Daublebsky, B.: Spielen in der Schule. Stuttgart, 1973.

Davis, Jessica Milner: Farce. Critical Idiom Series. London,1978.

Drögemüller, Hans-Peter: Handbuch für Studienreferendare. Stuttgart, 1977.

Ellis, Rod.: "Informal and formal approaches to communicative language
teaching". ELT Journal 36:2 (1982), S. 73-81.

Haven, Hans: Darstellendes Spiel. Funktionen und Formen. Düsseldorf, 1970.

Hoppe, Hans: "Theaterspielen als pädagogischer Erfahrungsraum".
In: Handbuch der Spielpädagogik Band 3. Herausgegeben von
Karl Josef Kreuzer. Düsseldorf, 1984, S. 313-32.

Jung, Udo O.H.: 'Holistische Methoden fremdsprachlicher Unterweisung als
Wegbereiter des neuen Schülertheaters. Eine Auswahlbibliographie".
Die Neueren Sprachen 85:1 (1986), S. 57-71.

Kluge, Norbert: Spielen und Erfahren. Der Zusammenhang von Spielerlebnis
und Lernprozeß. Bad Heilbrunn/Obb., 1981.

Der Kultusminister des Landes Nordrhein-Westfalen. Richtlinien für die
gymnasiale Oberstufe in Nordrhein-Westfalen: Englisch: Literaturkurse. Köln, 1981.

Lippert, Gerhard: "Spieldidaktische Positionen heute". In: A.O. Schorb,
Gertrud Simmerding (Hrsg.), Lehrerkolleg Spiel in der Schule.
München, 1980, S. 21-33.

Löffler, Renate: Spiele im Englischunterricht. Vom lehrergelenkten Lernspiel zum schülerorientierten Rollenspiel. München, Wien, Baltimore,
1979.

Löffler, Renate, Wulf-Michael Kunze: Spiele im Englischunterricht 2.
München, Wien, Baltimore, 1980.

Macht, Konrad, Hilde Arnold, Gerda Geppert, Rita Hösl: Das darstellende
Spiel im Englischunterricht. Ansbach, 1977.

Müller, Rudi: "Darstellendes Spiel im Fachunterricht der gymnasialen Oberstufe". In: Herbert Giffei (Hrsg.), Theater machen - Ein Handbuch
für die Amateur- und Schulbühne. Ravensburg, 1982, S. 368-380.

Newald, R.: "Vom Späthumanismus zur Empfindsamkeit".

In: Boor, H. de und R. Newald. Geschichte der Deutschen Literatur

Band 5. München, [3]1960.

Pflüger, Helmut: "Schüleraufführungen französischer Klassiker. Ein Mittel

zur Intensivierung des französischen Sprachgefühls". Praxis des

Neusprachlichen Unterrichts 13:2 (1966), S. 258-262.

Shaffer, Peter: Black Comedy. In: The Collected Plays of Peter Shaffer.

New York, 1982.

Stern, Susan L.: "Drama in Second Language Learning from a Psycholinguistic

Perspective". Language Learning 30:1 (1980), S. 77-100.

Taylor, John Russell: Peter Shaffer. Writers and their Work Series.

Harlow, 1974.

Trewin, J.C.: Peter Brook. A Biography. London, 1971.

Wode, Henning: Learning a Second Language. An Integrated View of

Language Acquisition. Tübingen, 1981.

Besetzung und Szeneneinteilung

CAST

Brindsley Miller	Silvia Kutscher
Carol Melkett	Nadja Bentz
Miss Furnival	Elke Kux (Nadja Hani)
Colonel Melkett	Ulrike Schmitt (Tatjana Rizzo)
Schuppanzigh	Isabel Schiffhorst
Clea	Kirsten Herrendorf
Bamberger	Anke Koch, Lutz Fröhmer

Souffleuse	Christiane Franzen, Anke Koch
Technik	Franz Schippers, Ingo Erken
Regie	Daniel Meyer-Dinkgräfe

SCENES

1 Brin, Carol
2 Brin, Carol, Miss Furnival
3 Brin, Carol, Miss Furnival, Colonel Melkett
4 Brin, Carol, Miss Furnival, Colonel Melkett, Harold Gorringe
5 Brin, Carol, Miss Furnival, Colonel Melkett, Harold Gorringe, Clea
6 Brin, Carol, Miss Furnival, Colonel Melkett, Harold Gorringe, Clea, Schuppanzigh
7 Brin, Carol, Miss Furnival, Colonel Melkett, Harold Gorringe, Clea
8 Brin, Carol, Colonel Melkett, Clea
9 Brin, Carol, Colonel Melkett, Clea, Harold Gorringe
10 Brin, Carol, Colonel Melkett, Clea, Harold Gorringe, Schuppanzigh, Bamberger

Telephone

Record-player

Chair
2

Brin's
sculpture

Sofa

Chair
3

Exit to
bedroom

Table

Budha

Exit to Brin's
studio

Exit to Harold's
flat

Chair
1

Drinks-
table

A U D I E N C E

Text von Peter Shaffers
Black Comedy

mit Strichen und zusätzlichen Regieanweisungen

THE SETTING

The action of the play takes place in BRINDSLEY's apartment in South Kensington, London. This forms the ground floor of a large house now divided into flats. HAROLD GORRINGE lives opposite; MISS FURNIVAL lives above. Right means stage right. Left means stage left.

There are four ways out of the room. A door at the left, upstage, leads directly across the passage to HAROLD's room. The door to this, with its mat laid tidily outside, can clearly be seen. A curtain, upstage center, screens BRINDSLEY's studio: when it is parted we glimpse samples of his work in metal. To the right of this an open stair shoots steeply up to his bedroom above, reached through a door at the top. To the left, downstage, a trap in the floor leads down to the cellar.

It is a gay room, when we finally see it, full of color and space and new shapes. It is littered with marvelous objects—mobiles, manikins, toys, and dotty bric-à-brac—the happy paraphernalia of a free and imaginative mind. The total effect is of chaos tidied in honor of an occasion, and of a temporary elegance created by the furniture borrowed from HAROLD GORRINGE and arranged to its best advantage.

This consists of three elegant Regency chairs in gold leaf; a Regency chaise longue to match; a small Queen Anne table bearing a fine opaline lamp, with a silk shade; a Wedgwood bowl in black basalt; a good Coalport vase containing summer flowers; and a fine porcelain Buddha.

The only things which actually belong to BRINDSLEY are a cheap square table bearing the drinks; an equally cheap round table in the middle of the room, shrouded by a cloth and decorated with the Wedgwood bowl; a low stool downstage center, improved by the Buddha; a record player; and his own artistic creations. These are largely assumed to be in the studio awaiting inspection; but one of them is visible in this room. On the dais stands a bizarre iron sculpture dominated by two long detachable metal prongs, and hung with metal pieces which jangle loudly if touched. On the wall hang paintings, some of them presumably by CLEA. All are nonfigurative: colorful geometric designs, splashes, splodges, and splats of color; whirls and whorls and wiggles—all testifying more to a delight in handling paint than to an ability to achieve very much with it.

THE TIME
9:30 on a Sunday night.

THE LIGHT
On the few occasions when a lighter is lit, matches are struck, or a torch is put on, the light on stage merely gets dimmer. When these objects are extinguished, the stage immediately grows brighter.

SCENE 1   [*Complete darkness. Two voices are heard:* BRINDSLEY *and* CAROL. *They must give the impression of two people walking round a room with absolute confidence, as if in the light. We hear sounds as of furniture being moved. A chair is dumped down.*]

1   BRINDSLEY: There! How do you think the room looks?

CAROL [*quacking*]: Fabulous! I wish you could always have it like this. That lamp looks divine there. And those chairs are just the right color. I told you green would look well in here.

BRINDSLEY: Suppose Harold comes back?

2   CAROL: He is not coming back till tomorrow morning.

[*We hear* BRINDSLEY *pacing nervously.*]

BRINDSLEY: I know. But suppose he comes tonight? He's mad about his antiques. What do you think he'll say if he goes into his room and finds out we've stolen them?

CAROL: Don't dramatize. We haven't stolen *all* his furniture. Just three chairs, the sofa, that table, the lamp, the bowl, and the vase of flowers, that's all.

BRINDSLEY: And the Buddha. That's more valuable than anything.

CAROL: Oh, do stop worrying, darling.

3   BRINDSLEY: Well, you don't know Harold. He won't even let anyone *touch* his antiques.

CAROL: Look, we'll put everything back as soon as Mr. Bamberger leaves. Now stop being dreary.

BRINDSLEY: Well, frankly, I don't think we should have done it. I mean— *anyway*, Harold or no.

CAROL: Why not, for heaven's sake? The room looks divine now. Just look at it!

BRINDSLEY: Darling, Georg Bamberger's a multimillionaire. He's lived all his life against this sort of furniture. Our few stolen bits aren't going to impress him. He's coming to see the work of an unknown sculptor. If you ask me, it would look much better to him if he found me exactly as I really am: a poor artist. It might touch his heart.

CAROL: It might—but it certainly won't impress Daddy. Remember, he's coming too.

BRINDSLEY: As if I could forget! Why you had to invite your monster father tonight, I can't think!

CAROL: Oh, not again!

BRINDSLEY: Well, it's too bloody much. If he's going to be persuaded I'm a fit husband for you, just by watching a famous collector buy some of my work, he doesn't deserve to have me as a son-in-law!

CAROL: He just wants some proof you can earn your own living.

BRINDSLEY: And what if Bamberger *doesn't* like my work?

CAROL: He will, darling. Just stop worrying.

4   BRINDSLEY: I can't. Get me a whisky.

[*She does. We hear her steps, and a glass clink against a bottle—~~then the sound of a soda syphon.~~*]

[*Grimly.*] I've got a foreboding. It's all going to be a disaster. An A1, copper-bottomed, twenty-four-carat disaster!

CAROL: Look, darling, you know what they say. Faint heart never won fair ladypegs!

BRINDSLEY: How true.

CAROL: The trouble with you is you're what Daddy calls a Determined Defeatist.

BRINDSLEY: The more I hear about your daddy, the more I hate him. I loathe military men anyway . . . and in any case, he's bound to hate me.

CAROL: Why?

BRINDSLEY: Because I'm a complete physical coward. He'll smell it on my breath.

CAROL: Look, darling, all you've got to do is stand up to him. Daddy's only a bully when he thinks people are afraid of him.

BRINDSLEY: Well, I am.

CAROL: You haven't even met him.

5   BRINDSLEY: That doesn't make any difference.

CAROL: Don't be ridiculous. [*Hands him a drink.*] Here.

BRINDSLEY: Thanks.

CAROL: What can he do to you?

BRINDSLEY: For one thing, he can refuse to let me marry you.

CAROL: Ah, that's sweetipegs!

[*We hear them embrace.*]

BRINDSLEY: I like you in yellow. It brings out your hair.

CAROL: Straighten your tie. You look sloppy.

BRINDSLEY: Well, you look divine.

CAROL: Really?

BRINDSLEY: I mean it. I've never seen you look so lovely.

CAROL: Tell me, Brin—have there been many before me?

BRINDSLEY: Thousands.

CAROL: Seriously!

BRINDSLEY: Seriously—none.

6 CAROL: What about that girl in the photo?

BRINDSLEY: She lasted about three months.

CAROL: When?

BRINDSLEY: Two years ago.

CAROL: What was her name?

BRINDSLEY: Clea.

CAROL: What was she like?

BRINDSLEY: She was a painter. Very honest. Very clever. And just about as cozy as a steel razor blade.

CAROL: When was the last time you saw her?

BRINDSLEY [*evasively*]: I told you . . . two years ago.

CAROL: Well, why did you still have her photo in your bedroom drawer?

BRINDSLEY: It was just there. That's all. Give me a kiss . . .[*Pause.*] No one in the world kisses like you.

CAROL [*murmuring*]: Tell me something. . . . Did you like it better with her—or me?

BRINDSLEY: Like what?

CAROL: Sexipegs.

BRINDSLEY: Look, people will be here in a minute. Put a record on. It had better be something for your father. What does he like?

7 CAROL [*crossing to the record player*]: He doesn't like anything except military marches.

BRINDSLEY: I might have guessed. . . . Wait—I think I've got some! That last record on the shelf. The orange cover. It's called "Marching and Murdering with Sousa," or something.

CAROL: This one?

BRINDSLEY: That's it.

CAROL [*getting it*]: "The Band of the Coldstream Guards."

BRINDSLEY: Ideal. Put it on.

CAROL: How'd you switch on?

8 BRINDSLEY: The last knob on the left. That's it. . . . Let us pray! . . . Oh, God, let this evening go all right! Let Mr. Bamberger like my sculpture and buy some! Let Carol's monster father like me! And let

9   my neighbor Harold Gorringe never find out that we borrowed his
precious furniture behind his back! Amen.

*[A Sousa march; loud. Hardly has it begun, however, when it runs down—
as if there is a failure of electricity. The sound stops.*

*Brilliant light floods the stage. The rest of the play, save for the times when
matches are struck or a flashlight is switched on, is acted in this light, but
as if in pitch darkness.*

They freeze: CAROL *by the end of the sofa;* BRINDSLEY *by the drinks table.
The girl's dress is a silk flag of chic wrapped round her greyhound's body.
The boy's look is equally cool: narrow, contained, and sexy. Throughout
the evening, as things slide into disaster for him, his crisp, detached shape
degenerates progressively into sweat and rumple—just as the elegance of his
room gives way relentlessly to its usual near-slum appearance. For the place,
as for its owner, the evening is a progress through disintegration.]*

God! We've blown a fuse!

[The structure and appearance of BRINDSLEY'S *room is described in the note
at the beginning of the play.]*

CAROL: Oh no!

10 BRINDSLEY: It must be. *[He blunders to the light switch, feeling ahead of him,
trying to part the darkness with his hands. Finding the switch, he flicks it
on and off.]*

CAROL: It is!

BRINDSLEY: Oh no!

CAROL: Or a power cut. Where's the box?

BRINDSLEY: In the hall.

CAROL: Have you any candles?

11 BRINDSLEY: No. Damn!

CAROL: Where are the matches?

12 BRINDSLEY: They should be on the drinks table. *[Feeling round the bottles]*
No. Try on the record player.

13 *[They both start groping about the room, feeling for matches.]*

Damn, damn, damn, damn, damn, damn!

*[*CAROL *sets a maraca rattling off the record player.]*

CAROL: There! *[Finding it.]* No . . .

[The telephone rings.]

14 BRINDSLEY: Would you believe it! *[He blunders his way toward the sound
of the bell. Just in time he remembers the central table—and stops himself
colliding into it with a smile of self-congratulation.]* All right: I'm coming!
~~[Instead he trips over the dais, and goes sprawling—knocking the phone onto
the floor. He has to grope for it on his knees, hauling the receiver back to him~~

~~by the wire~~. *Into receiver.*] Hello? . . . [*In sudden horror.*] *Hello!* . . . No, no, no, no—I'm fine, just fine! . . . You? . . . [*His hand over the receiver: to* CAROL.] Darling—look in the bedroom, will you?

CAROL: I haven't finished in here yet.

BRINDSLEY: Well, I've just remembered there's some fuse wire in the bedroom. In that drawer where you found the photograph. Go and get it, will you?

CAROL: I don't think there is. I didn't see any there.

BRINDSLEY [*snapping*]: Don't argue. Just look!

CAROL: All right. Keep your hairpiece on!

15   [*During the following she gropes her way cautiously up the stairs—head down, arms up the banisters, silken bottom thrust out with the effort.*]

BRINDSLEY [*controlling himself*]: I'm sorry. I just know it's there, that's all. You must have missed it.

CAROL: What about the matches?

BRINDSLEY: We'll have to mend it in the dark, that's all. Please hurry, dear.

CAROL [*climbing*]: Oh, God, how dreary! . . .

BRINDSLEY [*taking his hand off the receiver and listening to hear* CAROL *go*]: Hello? . . . Well, well, well, well! How are you? Good. That's just fine. Fine, fine! . . . Stop saying what?

[CAROL *reaches the top of the stairs—and from force of habit pulls down her skirt before groping her way into the bedroom.*]

BRINDSLEY [*hand still over the receiver*]: Carol? . . . Darling? . . . [*Satisfied she has gone; in a rush into the telephone, his voice low.*] Clea! What are you doing here? I thought you were in Finland. . . . But you've hardly been gone six weeks. . . . Where are you speaking from? . . . The air terminal? . . . Well, no, that's not a good idea tonight. I'm terribly busy, and I'm afraid I just can't get out of it. It's business.

CAROL [*calling from the bedroom door, above*]: There's nothing there except your dreary socks. I told you.

16   BRINDSLEY [*calling back*]: Well, try the other drawers! . . . [~~He rises as he speaks~~, *turning so that the wire wraps itself around his legs.*]

[CAROL *returns to her search.*]

[*Low and rapid, into phone.*]: Look: I can't talk now. Can I call you tomorrow? Where will you be? . . . Look, I told you *no*, Clea. Not tonight. I know it's just around the corner, that's not the point! You can't come round. . . . Look, the situation's changed. Something's happened this past month—

CAROL [*off*]: I can't see anything. Brin, *please!*

BRINDSLEY: Clea, I've got to go. . . . Look, I can't discuss it over the phone. . . . Has it got to do with what? Yes, of course it has. I mean you can't expect things to stay frozen, can you?

17   CAROL [*emerging from the bedroom*]: There's nothing here. Haven't we any matches at all?

BRINDSLEY: Oh, stop wailing! [*Into phone.*] No, not you. I'll call you tomorrow. Goodbye. [*He hangs up sharply—but fails to find the rest of the telephone so that he bangs the receiver hard on the table first. Then he has to disentangle himself from the wire. Already BRINDSLEY is beginning to be fussed.*]

18

CAROL [*descending*]: Who was that?

BRINDSLEY: Just a chum. Did you find the wire?

CAROL: I can't find anything in this. We've *got* to get some matches!

19   BRINDSLEY: I'll try the pub. Perhaps they'll have some candles as well.

SCENE 2

[*Little screams are heard approaching from above. It is MISS FURNIVAL groping her way down in a panic.*]

MISS FURNIVAL [*squealing*]: Help! Help! . . .Oh, please someone help me!

BRINDSLEY [*calling out*]: Is that you, Miss Furnival?

20   MISS FURNIVAL: Mr. Miller? . . .

BRINDSLEY: Yes?

MISS FURNIVAL: Mr. Miller!

BRINDSLEY: Yes!

[*She gropes her way in. BRINDSLEY crosses to find her, but narrowly misses her.*]

MISS FURNIVAL: Oh, thank God, you're there; I'm so frightened!

21   BRINDSLEY: Why? Have your lights gone too?

MISS FURNIVAL: Yes!

22   BRINDSLEY: It must be a power cut.

[*He finds her hand and leads her to the chair downstage left.*]

MISS FURNIVAL: I don't think so. The street lights are on in the front. I saw them from the landing.

BRINDSLEY: Then it must be the main switch of the house.

23   CAROL: Where is that?

[*MISS FURNIVAL gasps at the strange voice.*]

BRINDSLEY: It's in the cellar. It's all sealed up. No one's allowed to touch it but the electricity people.

CAROL: What are we going to do?

BRINDSLEY: Get them—quick!

24   CAROL: Will they come out at this time of night?

BRINDSLEY: They've got to.

[*BRINDSLEY accidentally touches MISS FURNIVAL's breasts. She gives a little scream.* BRINDSLEY *gropes his way to the phone.*]

Have you by any chance got a match on you, Miss Furnival?

MISS FURNIVAL: I'm afraid I haven't. So improvident of me. And I'm absolutely terrified of the dark!

BRINDSLEY: Darling, this is Miss Furnival, from upstairs. Miss Furnival— Miss Melkett.

MISS FURNIVAL: How do you do?

CAROL [*extending her hand in the darkness*]: How do you do?

25   MISS FURNIVAL: Isn't this frightful?

      [BRINDSLEY *picks up the phone and dials O.*]

CAROL: Perhaps we can put Mr. Bamberger off.

BRINDSLEY: Impossible. He's dining out and coming on here after. He can't be reached.

CAROL: Oh, flip!

26   BRINDSLEY [~~sitting on the dais, and~~ *speaking into the phone*]: Hello, Operator, can you give me the London Electricity Board, please? Night Service . . . I'm sure it's in the book, Miss, but I'm afraid I can't see. . . . There's no need to apologize. No, I'm not blind—I just can't see! We've got a fuse. . . . No, we *haven't* got any matches! [*Desperate.*] Miss, *please*: this is an emergency! . . . Thank you! . . . [*To the room.*] London is staffed with imbeciles!

MISS FURNIVAL: Oh, you're so right, Mr. Miller.

BRINDSLEY [~~rising~~, *frantic: into the phone*]: Miss, I *don't want* the number: I can't dial it! . . . Well, have *you* ever tried to dial a number in the dark? . . . [*Trying to keep control.*] I just want to be connected . . . thank you. [*To* MISS FURNIVAL] Miss Furnival, do you by any remote chance have any candles?

MISS FURNIVAL: I'm afraid not, Mr. Miller.

BRINDSLEY [*mouthing nastily at her*]: "I'm afraid not, Mr. Miller." . . . [*Briskly, into phone.*] Hello? Look, I'd like to report a main fuse at 18 Scarlatti Gardens. My name is Miller. [*Exasperated.*] Yes, yes! All right . . . ! [*Maddened: to the room.*] Hold on! Hold bloody on! . . .

MISS FURNIVAL: If I might suggest, Harold Gorringe opposite might have some candles. He's away for the weekend, but always leaves his key under the mat.

BRINDSLEY: What a good idea. That's just the sort of practical thing he would have. [*To* CAROL.] Here—take this . . . I'll go and see, love. [*He hands her the telephone in a fumble—then makes for the door—only to collide with his sculpture.*] Bugger!

27   MISS FURNIVAL: Are you all right, Mr. Miller?

BRINDSLEY: I knew it! I bloody knew it. This is going to be the worst night of my life! . . . [*He collides with the door.*]

CAROL: Don't panic, darling. Just don't panic!

[*He stumbles out ~~and is seen groping under~~ HAROLD's ~~mat for the key.~~ He ~~finds it and enters the room opposite.~~*]

MISS FURNIVAL: You're so right, Miss Melkett. We must none of us panic.

CAROL [*on the phone*]: Hello? Hello? [*To* MISS FURNIVAL.] This would have to happen tonight. It's just Brindsley's luck.

MISS FURNIVAL: Is it something special tonight then, Miss Melkett?

CAROL: It couldn't be more special if it tried.

MISS FURNIVAL: Oh dear. May I ask why?

CAROL: Have you ever heard of a German called Georg Bamberger?

MISS FURNIVAL: Indeed, yes. Isn't he the richest man in the world?

CAROL: Yes. [*Into phone.*] Hello? . . . [*To* MISS FURNIVAL.] Well, he's coming here tonight.

MISS FURNIVAL: Tonight!

CAROL: In about twenty minutes, to be exact. And to make matters worse, he's apparently stone deaf.

MISS FURNIVAL: How extraordinary! May I ask why he's coming?

CAROL: He saw some photos of Brindsley's work and apparently got madly excited about it. His secretary rang up last week and asked if he could come and see it. He's a great collector. Brin would be absolutely *made* if Bamberger bought a piece of his.

MISS FURNIVAL: Oh, how exciting!

CAROL: It's his big break. Or was—till a moment ago.

MISS FURNIVAL: Oh, my dear, you *must* get some help. Jiggle that thing.

CAROL [*jiggling the phone*]: Hello? Hello? . . . Perhaps the Bomb's fallen, and everyone's dead.

MISS FURNIVAL: Oh, please don't say things like that—even in levity.

CAROL [*someone answers her at last*]: Hello? Ah! This is Number 18, Scarlatti Gardens. I'm afraid we've had the most dreary fuse. It's what's laughingly known as the main switch. We want a *little man!* . . . Well, they can't *all* have flu . . . Oh, please try! It's screamingly urgent. . . . Thank you. [*She hangs up.*] Sometime this evening, they hope. That's a lot of help.

MISS FURNIVAL: They're not here to help, my dear. In my young days you paid your rates and you got satisfaction. Nowadays you just get some foreigner swearing at you. And if they think you're of the middle class, that only makes it worse.

CAROL: Would you like a drink?

MISS FURNIVAL: I don't drink, thank you. My dear father, being a Baptist minister, strongly disapproved of alcohol.

SCENE 3   29   [*A scuffle is heard among milk bottles off, followed by a stifled oath.*]

COLONEL MELKETT [*off*]: Damn and blast!! . . . [*Barking.*] Is there anybody there?

CAROL [*calling*]: In here, daddypegs!

COLONEL: Can't you put the light on, dammit? I've almost knocked meself out on a damn milk bottle.

CAROL: We've got a fuse. Nothing's working.

30   [COLONEL MELKETT *appears, holding a lighter which evidently is working— we can see the flame, and, of course, the lights go down a little.*]

MISS FURNIVAL: Oh, what a relief! A light!

31   CAROL: This is my father, Colonel Melkett, Miss Furnival. She's from upstairs.

COLONEL: Good evening.

MISS FURNIVAL: I'm taking refuge for a moment with Mr. Miller. I'm not very good in the dark.

COLONEL: When did this happen?

32   [MISS FURNIVAL. *glad for the light. follows it pathetically as the* COLONEL crosses the room.]

CAROL: Five minutes ago. The main just blew.

COLONEL: And where's this young man of yours?

CAROL: In the flat opposite. He's trying to find candles.

COLONEL: You mean he hasn't got any?

CAROL: No. We can't even find the matches.

COLONEL: I see. No organization. Bad sign!

CAROL: Daddy, please. It could happen to any of us.

33   COLONEL: Not to me.

[*He turns to find* MISS FURNIVAL *right behind him and glares at her balefully. The poor woman retreats to the sofa and sits down.*]

34   [COLONEL MELKETT *gets his first sight of* BRINDSLEY'*s sculpture.*] What the hell's that?

CAROL: Some of Brindsley's work.

COLONEL: Is it, by Jove? And how much does that cost?

CAROL: I think he's asking fifty pounds for it.

COLONEL: My God!

CAROL [*nervously*]: Do you like the flat, Daddy? He's furnished it very well, hasn't he? I mean it's rich, but not gaudipegs.

35   COLONEL: Very elegant—good: I can see he's got excellent taste. [*Seeing the Buddha*] Now that's what I understand by a real work of art—you can see what it's meant to be.

MISS FURNIVAL: Good heavens!

CAROL: What is it?

MISS FURNIVAL: Nothing . . . it's just that Buddha—it so closely resembles the one Harold Gorringe has.

[CAROL *looks panic-stricken.*]

COLONEL: It must have cost a pretty penny, what? He must be quite well off. . . . By Jove—it's got pretty colors. [*He bends to examine it.*]

CAROL [*sotto voce, urgently, to* MISS FURNIVAL]: You *know* Mr. Gorringe?

MISS FURNIVAL: Oh, very well indeed! We're excellent friends. He has such lovely things . . . [*For the first time she notices the sofa on which she is sitting*] Oh . . .

CAROL: What?

MISS FURNIVAL: This furniture . . . [*Looking about her.*] Surely?—my goodness!

CAROL [*hastily*]: Daddy, why don't you look in there? It's Brin's studio.
36   There's something I particularly want you to see before he comes back.

COLONEL: What?

CAROL: It—it—er—it's a surprise, go and see.

COLONEL: Very well, Dumpling. Anythin' to oblige. [*To* MISS FURNIVAL.] Excuse me.

[*He goes off into the studio, taking his lighter with him. The light instantly gets brighter on stage.* CAROL *sits beside the spinster on the sofa, crouching like a conspirator.*]

37   CAROL [*low and urgent*]: Miss Furnival, you're a sport, aren't you?

MISS FURNIVAL: I don't know. What is this furniture doing in here? It belongs to Harold Gorringe.

CAROL: I know. We've done something absolutely frightful. We've stolen all his best pieces and put Brin's horrid old bits in *his* room.

MISS FURNIVAL: But why? It's disgraceful!

CAROL [*sentimentally*]: Because Brindsley's got nothing. Miss Furnival. Nothing at all. He's as poor as a churchmouse. If Daddy had seen this place as it looks normally, he'd have forbidden our marriage on the spot. Mr. Gorringe wasn't there to ask—so we just took the chance.

MISS FURNIVAL: If Harold Gorringe knew that anyone had touched his furniture or his porcelain, he'd go out of his mind! And as for that Buddha—[*pointing in the wrong direction*] it's the most precious piece he owns. It's worth hundreds of pounds.

CAROL: Oh, please, Miss Furnival—you won't give us away, will you? We're desperate! And it's only for an hour. . . . Oh, please! *please!*

MISS FURNIVAL [*giggling*]: Very well! . . . I won't betray you!

38   CAROL: Oh, thank you!

MISS FURNIVAL: But it'll have to go back exactly as it was, just as soor as Mr. Bamberger and your father leave.

CAROL: I swear! Oh, Miss Furnival, you're an angel! Do have a drink. Oh, no, you don't. Well, have a bitter lemon.

39   MISS FURNIVAL: Thank you. That I won't refuse.

[*The* COLONEL *returns, still holding his lighter. The stage darkens a little.*]

COLONEL: Well, they're certainly a surprise. And that's supposed to be sculpture?

CAROL: It's not supposed to be. It is.

COLONEL: They'd make good garden implements. I'd like 'em for turnin' the soil.

[MISS FURNIVAL *giggles.*]

CAROL: That's not very funny, Daddy.

[MISS FURNIVAL *stops giggling.*]

COLONEL: Sorry, Dumpling. Speak as you find.

CAROL: I wish you wouldn't call me Dumpling.

COLONEL: Well, there's no point wastin' this. We may need it!

[*He snaps off his lighter.* MISS FURNIVAL *gives her little gasp as the stage brightens.*]

CAROL: Don't be nervous, Miss Furnival. Brin will be here in a minute with the candles.

MISS FURNIVAL: Then I'll leave, of course. I don't want to be in your way.

CAROL: You're not at all. [*Hearing him.*] Brin?

40   [BRINDSLEY ~~comes out of HAROLD's room—returns the key under the mat.~~]

BRINDSLEY: Hello?

CAROL: Did you find anything?

BRINDSLEY ~~[coming in]~~. You can't find anything in this! If there's candles there, *I* don't know where they are. Did you get the electric people?

CAROL: They said they might send someone around later.

41   BRINDSLEY: How much later?

CAROL: They don't know.

BRINDSLEY: That's a lot of help. What a lookout! Not a bloody candle in the house. A deaf millionaire to show sculpture to—and your monster father to keep happy. Lovely!

COLONEL [*grimly lighting his lighter*]: Good evenin'.

[BRINDSLEY *jumps.*]

CAROL: Brin, this *is* my father—Colonel Melkett.

BRINDSLEY [*wildly embarrassed*]: Well, well, well, well, well! . . . [*Panic.*] Good evening, sir. Fancy you being there all the time! I—I'm expecting

some dreadful neighbors, some neighbor monsters, monster neighbors,
you know. . . . They rang up and said they might look round . . .
Well, well, well! . . .

COLONEL [*darkly*]: Well, well.

MISS FURNIVAL [*nervously*]: Well, well!

42   CAROL [*brightly*]: Well!

      [*The* COLONEL ~~rises and~~ *advances on* BRINDSLEY, *who retreats before him
across the room.*]

COLONEL: You seem to be in a spot of trouble.

BRINDSLEY [*with mad nervousness*]: Oh, not really! Just a fuse—nothing
really, we have them all the time . . . I mean, it won't be the first
fuse I've survived, and I dare say it won't be the last! [*He gives a wild
braying laugh.*]

COLONEL [*relentless*]: In the meantime, you've got no matches. Right?

BRINDSLEY: Right.

COLONEL: No candles. Right?

BRINDSLEY: Right.

COLONEL: No basic efficiency, right?

BRINDSLEY: I wouldn't say that, exactly . . .

43   COLONEL: By basic efficiency, young man, I mean the simple state of
being At Attention in life, rather than At Ease. Understand?

BRINDSLEY: Well, I'm certainly not at ease.

COLONEL: What are you goin' to do about it?

BRINDSLEY: Do?

COLONEL: Don't echo me, sir. I don't like it.

BRINDSLEY: You don't like it . . . I'm sorry.

44   COLONEL: Now look you here. This is an emergency. Anyone can see
that.

BRINDSLEY: No one can see anything: that's the emergency! [*He gives his
braying laugh again.*]

COLONEL: Spare me your humor, sir, if you don't mind. Let's look at the
situation objectively. Right?

BRINDSLEY: Right.

COLONEL: Good. [*He snaps off the lighter.*] Problem: Darkness. Solution:
Light.

BRINDSLEY: Oh, very good, sir.

COLONEL: Weapons: Matches: none! Candles: none! What remains?

45   BRINDSLEY: Search me.

COLONEL [*triumphantly*]: Torches. Torches, sir! what?

BRINDSLEY: Or a set of early Christians.

COLONEL: What did you say?

BRINDSLEY: I'm sorry. I think I'm becoming unhinged. Very good. Torches—brilliant.

COLONEL: Routine. Well, where would you find one?

BRINDSLEY: The pub. What time is it?

[*The* COLONEL *lights his lighter, but now not at the first try. The stage lights flickers up and down accordingly.*]

COLONEL: Blasted thing. It's beginnin' to go. [*He consults his watch.*] Quarter to ten. You can just make it, if you hurry.

46   BRINDSLEY: Thank you, sir. Your clarity of mind has saved the day!

COLONEL: Well, get on with it, man.

BRINDSLEY: Yes, sir! Back in a minute!

47   [*The* COLONEL *sits in the Regency chair, downstage right.*]

CAROL: Good luck, darling.

BRINDSLEY: Thank you, my sweet.

[*She blows him a kiss. He blows her one back.*]

SCENE 4   COLONEL [*irritated*]: Stop that at once!

[BRINDSLEY *starts for the door, but as he reaches it,* HAROLD GORRINGE *is heard, off.*]

HAROLD [~~~~]: Hello? Hello? Anyone there?

BRINDSLEY [*freezing with horror*]: HAROLD!!

HAROLD: Brindsley?

BRINDSLEY [*meant for* CAROL]: It's Harold! He's back!

CAROL: Oh no!

BRINDSLEY: THE FURNITURE!!

HAROLD: What's going on here?

[HAROLD *appears. He wears a smart raincoat and carries a weekend suitcase. His hair falls over his brow in a flossy attempt at elegance.*]

BRINDSLEY: Nothing, Harold. Don't go in there—come in here! We've had a fuse. It's dark—it's all over the house.

HAROLD: Have you phoned the electric? [*Reaching out.*]

BRINDSLEY [*reaching out and grabbing him*]: Yes. Come in here.

48   HAROLD [*grabbed*]: Ohh! . . . [*He takes* BRINDSLEY's *hand and enters the room cozily on his arm.*] It's rather cozy in the dark, isn't it?

BRINDSLEY [*desperately*]: Yes! I suppose so. . . . So, you're back from your weekend then . . .

HAROLD: I certainly am, dear. Weekend! Some weekend! It rained the whole bloody time. I feel damp to my knickers.

BRINDSLEY [*nervously*]: Well, have a drink and tell us all about it.

49   HAROLD: Us? [*Disengaging himself.*] Who's here, then?

MISS FURNIVAL [archly]: I am, Mr. Gorringe.

HAROLD: Ferny?

MISS FURNIVAL: Taking refuge, I'm afraid. You know how I hate the dark.

COLONEL [attempting to light his lighter]: Blasted thing! . . . [He succeeds.] There we are! [Raising it to GORRINGE's face, with distaste.] Who are you?

BRINDSLEY: May I present my neighbor. This is Harold Gorringe—Colonel Melkett.

HAROLD: How do?

COLONEL: How d'ye do?

BRINDSLEY: And this is Carol Melkett, Harold Gorringe.

CAROL [giving him a chilly smile]: Hello!? . . .

[HAROLD nods coldly.]

BRINDSLEY: Here, let me take your raincoat, Harold.

HAROLD [taking it off and handing it to him]: Be careful, it's sopping wet. [He is wearing a tight, modish, gray suit and a brilliant strawberry shirt. Adroitly, BRINDSLEY drops the raincoat over the Wedgwood bowl on the table.]

COLONEL: You've got no candles, I suppose?

50 HAROLD: Would you believe it, Colonel, but I haven't! Silly me!

[BRINDSLEY crosses and blows out the COLONEL's lighter, just as HAROLD begins to look around the room. The stage brightens.]

COLONEL: What the devil did you do that for?

BRINDSLEY: I'm saving your wick, Colonel. You may need it later and it's failing fast.

[The COLONEL gives him a suspicious look. BRINDSLEY moves quickly back,

51 takes up the coat and drops it over the right end of the sofa, to conceal as much of it as possible.]

HAROLD: It's all right. I've got some matches.

CAROL [alarmed]: Matches!

HAROLD: Here we are! I hope I've got the right end. [He strikes one.]

[BRINDSLEY immediately blows it out from behind, then moves swiftly to hide the Wedgwood bowl under the table and drop the tablecloth over the remaining end of the sofa. MISS FURNIVAL sits serenely unknowing between the two covers.]

Hey, what was that?

BRINDSLEY [babbling]: A draft. No match stays alight in this room. It's impossible. Crosscurrents, you know! Old houses are full of them. They're almost a permanent feature in this house. . . .

52 HAROLD [bewildered]: I don't know what you're on about. [He strikes another match.]

[BRINDSLEY *agains blows it out as he nips over to sit in the chair downstage left, but this time is seen.*]

HAROLD: What's up with you?

BRINDSLEY: Nothing!

HAROLD: Have you got a dead body in here or something?

BRINDSLEY: NO! [*He starts his maniacal laughter.*]

HAROLD: Here, have you been drinking?

BRINDSLEY: No. Of course not.

[HAROLD *strikes another match.* BRINDSLEY *dashes up to him and yet again blows it out. All these strikings and blowings are of course accompanied by swift and violent alterations of the light.*]

HAROLD [*exasperated*]: Now look here! What's up with you?

BRINDSLEY [*inspired*]: Dangerous!

HAROLD: What?

BRINDSLEY [*frantically improvising*]: Dangerous! It's dangerous! . . . We can all die! . . . Naked flames! Hideous accidents can happen with naked flames!

HAROLD: I don't know what you're on about—what's up with you?

[BRINDSLEY *clutches* HAROLD *and backs him bewilderedly across to the center table.*]

BRINDSLEY: I've just remembered! It's something they always warn you about. In old houses the fuse box and the gas meter are in the same cupboard. They are here!

COLONEL: So what about it?

BRINDSLEY: Well . . . electrical blowouts can damage the gas supply. They're famous for it! They do it all the time! And they say you've got to avoid naked flames till they're mended.

53 COLONEL [*suspicious*]: I've never heard of that.

HAROLD: Me neither.

BRINDSLEY: Well, take my word for it. It's fantastically dangerous to burn naked flames in this room!

CAROL [*catching on*]: Brin's absolutely right. In fact, they warned me about it on the phone this evening when I called them. They said, "Whatever you do, don't strike a match till the fuse is mended."

BRINDSLEY: There, you see!—it's terribly dangerous.

COLONEL [*grimly*]: Then why didn't you warn me, Dumpling?

CAROL: I—I forgot.

COLONEL: Brilliant!

MISS FURNIVAL: Oh, goodness, we must take care!

BRINDSLEY: We certainly must! . . . [*Pause.*] Let's all have a drink. Cheer us up! . . .

CAROL: Good idea! Mr. Gorringe, would you like a drink?

HAROLD: Well, I must say, that wouldn't come amiss. Not after the journey I've had tonight. I swear to God there was thirty-five people in that compartment if there was one—babes in arms, toddlers, two nuns, three yapping poodles, and not a sausage to eat from Leamington to London. It's a bloody disgrace.

MISS FURNIVAL: You'd think they'd put on a restaurnat car, Mr. Gorringe.

HAROLD: Not them, Ferny. They don't care if you perish once they've got your fare. Excuse me. I'll just go and clean up.

BRINDSLEY [panic]: You can do that here!

HAROLD: Well, I must unpack anyway.

BRINDSLEY: Do it later.

HAROLD: No, I hate to keep clothes in a suitcase longer than I absolutely have to. If there's one thing I can't stand, it's a creased suit.

BRINDSLEY: Five more minutes won't hurt, surely?

HAROLD: Ooh, you aren't half bossy!

CAROL: What will you have? Winnie, Vera, or Ginette?

HAROLD: Come again?

CAROL: Winnie Whisky, Vera Vodka, or dear old standby Ginette.

HAROLD [yielding]: I can see you're the camp one! . . . If it's all the same to you, I'll have a drop of Ginette, please, and a little lime juice.

COLONEL [irritated]: Young man, do I have to keep reminding you that you are in an emergency? You have a guest arrivin' any second.

BRINDSLEY: Oh, God, I'd forgotten!

COLONEL: Try the pub. Try the neighbor's. Try who you damn well please, sir—but get a torch!

BRINDSLEY: Yes . . . yes! . . . [Airily.] Carol, can I have a word with you, please?

CAROL: I'm here.

[She gropes toward him and BRINDSLEY leads her to the stairs.]

COLONEL: What now?

BRINDSLEY: Excuse us just a moment, please. Colonel.

[He pulls her quickly after him, up the stairs.]

MISS FURNIVAL [as they do this]: Oh, Mr. Gorringe, it's so exciting. You'll never guess who's coming here tonight.

HAROLD: Who?

MISS FURNIVAL: Guess.

HAROLD: The Queen!

MISS FURNIVAL: Oh, Mr. Gorringe, you are ridiculous!

54 [BRINDSLEY arrives at the top of the stairs, then opens the bedroom door and closes it behind them.]

BRINDSLEY: What are we going to do?

CAROL [behind the door]: I don't know!

BRINDSLEY [behind the door]: Think!

CAROL: But—

BRINDSLEY: Think!

COLONEL: Is that boy touched or somethin'?

HAROLD: Touched? He's an absolute poppet.

COLONEL: A what?

HAROLD: A duck. I've known him for years, ever since he came here. There's not many secrets we keep from each other, I can tell you.

COLONEL [frostily]: Really?

HAROLD: Yes, really. He's a very sweet boy.

55   [BRINDSLEY and CAROL emerge from behind the bedroom door.]

BRINDSLEY: We'll have to put all Harold's furniture back in his room.

CAROL: Now?!

BRINDSLEY: We'll have to! I can't get a torch till we do.

CAROL: We can't!

BRINDSLEY: We must. He'll go mad if he finds out what we've done!

HAROLD: Well, come on, Ferny: don't be a tease. Who is it? Who's coming?

MISS FURNIVAL: I'll give you a clue. It's someone with money.

HAROLD: Money? . . . Let me think.

COLONEL [calling out]: Carol!

CAROL: Look, can't you just tell him it was a joke?

BRINDSLEY: You don't know him. He can't bear anyone to touch his treasures. They're like children to him. He cleans everything twice a day with a special swansdown duster. He'd wreck everything. Would you like him to call me a thief in front of your father?

CAROL: Of course not!

BRINDSLEY: Well, he would. He gets absolutely hysterical. I've seen him.

COLONEL: Brindsley!

CAROL: Well, how the hell can we do it?

HAROLD: It's no good. You can't hear up there.

BRINDSLEY [stripping off his jacket]: Look, you hold the fort. Serve them drinks. Just keep things going. Leave it all to me. I'll try and put everything back in the dark.

CAROL: It won't work.

BRINDSLEY: It's got to!

COLONEL
56
COLONEL CAROL [roaring]: Brindsley!!

BRINDSLEY [dashing to the door]: Coming, sir. . . .[With false calm.] I'm just getting some empties to take to the pub.

57 COLONEL: Say what you like. That boy's touched.
BRINDSLEY [*to* CAROL, *intimately*]: Trust me, darling.
[*They kiss.*]
COLONEL: At the double, Miller.
BRINDSLEY: Yes, sir! Yes, sir! [*He rushes out ~~and in his anxiety he misses his~~ ~~footing and falls neatly down the entire flight of stairs. Picking himself up.~~*]
I'm off now, Colonel! Help is definitely on the way.
COLONEL: Well, hurry it up, man.
BRINDSLEY: Carol will give you drinks. If Mr. Bamberger arrives, just explain the situation to him.

58 HAROLD [*feeling for his hand*]: Would you like me to come with you?
BRINDSLEY: No, no, no—good heavens: stay and enjoy yourself!
[HAROLD *kisses his hand.* BRINDSLEY *pulls it away.*]

59 I mean, you must be exhausted after all those poodles. A nice gin and lime will do wonders for you. I shan't be a minute. [*He reaches the door, opens it, then slams it loudly, remaining on the inside. Stealthily he opens it again, stands dead still for a moment, center, silently indicating to himself the position of the chairs he has to move—then he finds his way to the first of the Regency chairs, downstage left, which he lifts noiselessly.*]
CAROL [*with bright desperation*]: Well now, drinks! What's everyone going

60 to have? It's Ginette for Mr. Gorringe and I suppose Winnie for Daddy.
COLONEL: And how on earth are you going to do that in the dark?
CAROL: I remember the exact way I put out the bottles.
[BRINDSLEY *bumps into her with the chair and falls back, gored by its leg.*]
CAROL: It's very simple.
HAROLD: Oh, look, luv, let me strike a match. I'm sure it's not that dangerous, just for a *minute!* [*He strikes a match.*]
CAROL: Oh no! . . .

61 [BRINDSLEY *ducks down, chair in hand, and Carol blows out the match.*]
Do you want to blow us all up, Mr. Gorringe? . . . All poor Mr. Bamberger would find would be teensy-weensy bits of us. Very messypegs!
[*She snatches the box of matches, feels for the ice bucket, and drops them into it.* BRINDSLEY *steals out, Felix-the-cat-like, with the chair as* CAROL *fumblingly starts to mix drinks. He sets it down, opens* HAROLD'*s door, and disappears inside it with the chair.*]
HAROLD: Bamberger? Is that who's coming? Georg Bamberger?
MISS FURNIVAL: Yes. To see Mr. Miller's work. Isn't it exciting?
HAROLD: Well, I never! I read an article about him last week in the

62 Sunday paper. He's known as the mystery millionaire. ⁄He's almost

completely deaf—deaf as a post—and spends most of his time indoors
alone with his collection. He hardly ever goes out, except to a gallery
or a private studio. That's the life! If I had money that's what I'd do.
Just collect all the china and porcelain I wanted.

[BRINDSLEY *returns with a poor, broken-down chair of his own and sets it
down in the same position as the one he has taken out. The second chair
presents a harder challenge. It sits right across the room, upstage right.
Delicately he moves toward it—but he has difficulty finding it. We watch
him walk round and round it in desperately narrowing circles till he touches
it and with relief picks it up.*]

MISS FURNIVAL: I've never met a millionaire. I've always wondered if they
feel different to us. I mean their actual skins.

COLONEL: Their skins?

MISS FURNIVAL: Yes. I've always imagined they must be softer than ours.
Like the skins of ladies when I was a girl.

CAROL: What an interesting idea.

HAROLD: Oh, she's very fanciful is Ferny. Real imagination, I always say.

MISS FURNIVAL: Very kind of you, Mr. Gorringe. You're always so generous
with your compliments.

[*As she speaks her next speech staring smugly into the darkness, hands clasped
in maidenly gentility, the second Regency chair is being moved slowly across
what should be her field of vision, two inches from her face. During the
following,* BRINDSLEY *unfortunately misaims and carries the chair past the
door, bumps into the wall, retreats from it, and inadvertently shuts the door
softly with his back. Now he cannot get out of the room. He has to set down
the chair, grope for the door handle, turn it, then open the door—then refind
the chair, which he has quite lost. This takes a long and frantic time. At
last he triumphs, and staggers from the room, nearly exhausted.*]

But this is by no means fancy. In my day, softness of skin was quite
the sign of refinement. Nowadays, of course, it's hard enough for us
middle classes to keep ourselves decently clothed, let alone soft. My
father used to say, even before the bombs came and burned our dear
little house at Wendover: 'The game's up, my girl. We middle classes
are as dead as the dodo.' Poor Father, how right he was.

[Note: *Hopefully, if the counterpoint of farce action goes well,* MISS
FURNIVAL *may have to ad-lib a fair bit during all this, and not mind too
much if nobody hears her. The essential thing for all four actors during the
furniture moving is to preserve the look of ordinary conversation.*]

COLONEL: Your father was a professional man?

MISS FURNIVAL: He was a man of God, Colonel.

COLONEL: Oh.

66 [BRINDSLEY *returns with a broken-down rocking chair of his own. He crosses gingerly to where the* COLONEL *is sitting.*]

How are those drinks coming, Dumpling?

67 CAROL: Fine, Daddy. They'll be one minute.

COLONEL [*speaking directly into* BRINDSLEY's *face*]: Let me help you.

[BRINDSLEY *staggers back, startled.*]

CAROL: You can take this bitter lemon to Miss Furnival if you want.

[BRINDSLEY *sets down the rocker immediately next to the* COLONEL's *chair.*]

COLONEL: Very well.

[*He rises just as* BRINDSLEY's *hand pulls it from beneath him. With his other hand* BRINDSLEY *pulls the rocker into the identical position. The* COLONEL *moves slowly across the room, arms outstretched for the bitter lemon. Unknowingly* BRINDSLEY *follows him, carrying the third chair. The* COLONEL *collides gently with the table. At the same moment* BRINDSLEY *reaches it*

68 *upstage of him, and searches for the Wedgwood bowl. Their hands narrowly miss. Then* BRINDSLEY *remembers the bowl is under the table. Deftly he reaches down and retrieves it—and carrying it in one hand and the chair in the other, triumphantly leaves the room through the arch unconsciously provided by the outstretched arms of* CAROL *and the* COLONEL, *giving and receiving a glass of Scotch—which they think is lemonade.*]

69 CAROL: Here you are, Daddy. Bitter lemon for Miss Furnival.

COLONEL: Right you are, Dumpling. [*To* MISS FURNIVAL.] So your father was a minister, then?

MISS FURNIVAL: He was a saint, Colonel. I'm only thankful he never lived to see the rudeness and vulgarity of life today.

[*The* COLONEL *sets off to find her but goes much too far to the right.*]

HAROLD [*sits on the sofa beside her*]: Oooh, you're so right, Ferny. Rudeness and vulgarity—that's it to a T. The manners of some people today are beyond belief. Honestly. Did I tell you what happened in my shop last Friday? I don't think I did.

MISS FURNIVAL: No, Mr. Gorringe, I don't think so.

[*Her voice corrects the* COLONEL's *direction. During the following he moves slowly up toward her.*]

HAROLD: Well, I'd just opened up—it was about quarter to ten and I was dusting off the teapots—you know, Rockingham collects the dust something shocking!—when who should walk in but that Mrs. Levitt, you know—the ginger-haired bit I told you about, the one who thinks she's God's gift to bachelors.

COLONEL [*finding her head with his hand and presenting her with the Scotch*]: Here's your lemonade.

MISS FURNIVAL: Oh, thank you. Most kind.

[Throughout HAROLD's *story,* MISS FURNIVAL *nurses the glass, not drinking. The* COLONEL *finds his way slowly back to the chair he thinks he was sitting on before, but which is now a rocker.* BRINDSLEY *reappears triumphantly carrying one of the original Regency chairs he took out. He moves slowly across the room getting his bearings.]*

70 HAROLD: Anyway, she's got in her hand a vase I'd sold her last week— it was a birthday present for an old geezer she's having a bit of a ding- dong with somewhere in Earl's Court, hoping to collect all his lolly when he dies, as I read the situation. I'm a pretty good judge of character, Ferny, as you know—and she's a real grasper if ever I saw one.

[The COLONEL *sits heavily in the rocking chair which overbalances backwards, spilling him onto the floor.]*

COLONEL: Dammit to hell!

71 CAROL: What's the matter, Daddy?

[A pause. BRINDSLEY *sits down panic-stricken on the chair he has carried in. The* COLONEL *feels the chair and sets it on its feet.]*

COLONEL *[unbelieving]*: It's a blasted rockin' chair! I didn't see a blasted rockin' chair here before! . . .

72 *[Astounded, the* COLONEL *remains on the floor.* BRINDSLEY *rises and moves the chair to the original position of the second chair he moved.]*

HAROLD: Oh yes, you want to watch that. It's in a pretty ropey condition. I've told Brin about it several times. Anyway, this vase. It's a nice bit of Kang Tsi, blue and white with a good orange-peel glaze, absolutely authentic—I'd let her have it for forty-five pounds, and she'd got infinitely the best of the bargain, no arguments about that!

73 *[HAROLD *rises and leans against the center table to tell his story more effectively. The* COLONEL *seats himself again, gingerly.]*

Well, in she prances, her hair all done up in one of them bouffon hair- dos, you know, tarty—French-like—it would have looked fancy on a girl half her age with twice her looks—

*[BRINDSLEY *mistakenly lifts the end of the sofa.* MISS FURNIVAL *gives a little scream at the jolt.]*

HAROLD: Exactly! You know the sort.

*[BRINDSLEY *staggers in the opposite direction downstage onto the rostrum.]*

And d'you know what she says to me? "Mr. Gorringe," she says, "I've been cheated."

MISS FURNIVAL: No!

HAROLD: Her very words. "Cheated."

*[BRINDSLEY *collides with the sculpture on the dais. It jangles violently.]*

[*To it.*] Hush up, I'm talking!

74   CAROL [*covering up*]: I'm frightfully sorry.

[HAROLD *whirls round, surprised.*]

75   HAROLD: Anyway—"Oh," I say, "and how exactly has that occurred, Mrs. Levitt?" "Well," she says, "quite by chance I took this vase over to Bill Everett in the Portobello, and he says it's not what you called it at all, Chinese and very rare. He says it's a piece of nineteenth-century English trash!"

[BRINDSLEY *finds the lamp on the downstage table and picks it up. He walks with it round the rocking chair, on which the* COLONEL *is now sitting again.*]

"Does he?" I say. "Does he?" I keep calm. I always do when I'm riled. "Yes," she says. "He does. And I'd thank you to give me my money

76   back!"

[*The wire of the lamp has followed* BRINDSLEY *round the bottom of the rocking chair. It catches.* BRINDSLEY *tugs it gently. The chair moves. Surprised, the* COLONEL *jerks forward.* BRINDSLEY *tugs it again, much harder. The rocking chair is pulled forward, spilling the* COLONEL *out of it, again onto the floor, and then falling itself on top of him. The shade of the lamp comes off. During the ensuing dialogue* BRINDSLEY *gets to his knees and crawls right across the room following the flex of the lamp. He finds the plug, pulls it out, and—still on his knees—retraces his steps, winding up the wire around his arm, and becoming helplessly entangled in it. The* COLONEL *remains on the floor, now really alarmed.*]

77   MISS FURNIVAL: How dreadful, Mr. Gorringe. What did you do?

HAROLD: I counted to ten, and then I let her have it. "In the first place,"

78   I said, "I don't expect my customers to go checking up on my honesty behind my back. In the second, Bill Everett is ignorant as Barnsley dirt; he doesn't know Tang from Ting. And in the third place, that applies to you, too, Mrs. Levitt."

MISS FURNIVAL: You didn't!

HAROLD: I certainly did—and worse than that. "You've got in your hand," I said, "a minor masterpiece of Chinese pottery. But in point of fact," I said, "you're not even fit to hold a 1953 Coronation mug.

79   Don't you ever come in here again," I said, "don't you cross my threshold. Because, if you do, Mrs. Levitt, I won't make myself responsible for the consequences."

CAROL [*with two drinks in her hand*]: My, Mr. Gorringe, how splendid of you. Here's your gin and lime. You deserve it. [*She hands him the bitter lemon.*]

HAROLD [*accepting it*]: Ta. I was proper blazing, I didn't care!

CAROL: Where are you? Where are you, Daddy? Here's your Scotch.

COLONEL: Here, Dumpling!

80   [*He gets up dazedly and fumbles his way to the glass of gin and lime. BRINDSLEY meanwhile realizes he has lost the shade of the lamp. On his knees, he begins to look for it.*]

HAROLD: Carroty old bitch— telling *me* about pottery! *Oooh!!* [*He shakes himself indignantly at the recollection of it.*]

MISS FURNIVAL: Do you care for porcelain yourself, Colonel?

COLONEL: I'm afraid I don't know very much about it, madam. I like some of that Chinese stuff—you get some lovely colors, like on that

81   statue I saw when I came in here—very delicate.

HAROLD: What statue's that, Colonel?

COLONEL: The one on the packing case, sir. Very fine.

HAROLD: I didn't know Brin had any Chinese stuff. What's it of then, this statue?

       [BRINDSLEY *freezes.*]

CAROL [*desperately*]: Well, we've all got drinks, I'd like to propose Daddy's regimental toast. Raise your glasses everyone! "To the dear old Twenty-fifth Horse. Up the British, and Down with the Enemy!"

MISS FURNIVAL: I'll drink to that! Up the British!

HAROLD: Up the old Twenty-fifth!!

       [*Quickly* BRINDSLEY *finds the Buddha, moves it from the packing case to the table, then gets* HAROLD's *raincoat from the sofa, and wraps the statue up in it, leaving it on the table.*]

COLONEL: Thank you, Dumpling. That was very touchin' of you. Very touchin' indeed. [*He swallows his drink.*] Dammit, that's gin!

HAROLD: I've got lemonade!

MISS FURNIVAL: Oh! Horrible! . . .Quite horrible! That would be alcohol, I suppose! . . .Oh dear, how unpleasant! . . .

HAROLD [*to* MISS FURNIVAL]: Here, luv, exchange with me. No—you get the lemonade—but I get the gin. Colonel—

COLONEL: Here, sir.

       [*Seizing her chance* MISS FURNIVAL *downs a huge draft of Scotch. They all exchange drinks.* BRINDSLEY *resumes his frantic search for the shade.*]

HAROLD: Here, Ferny.

82   [*The* COLONEL *hands her the gin and lime. He gets instead the bitter lemon from* HAROLD. HAROLD *gets the Scotch.*]

MISS FURNIVAL: Thank you.

HAROLD: Well, let's try again. Bottoms up!

COLONEL: Quite.

[*They drink. Triumphantly,* BRINDSLEY *finds the shade. Unfortunately at the same moment the* COLONEL *spits out his lemonade in a fury all over him, as he marches toward him on his knees.*]

Look here—I can't stand another minute of this! [*He fishes his lighter out of his pocket and angrily tries to light it.*]

CAROL: Daddy, please!

COLONEL: I don't care, Dumpling. If I blow us up, then I'll blow us up! This is *ridiculous!* . . .

[*His words die in the flame. He spies* BRINDSLEY *kneeling at his feet, wound about with lamp wire.*]

What the devil are you doin' there?

BRINDSLEY [*blowing out his lighter*]: Now don't be rash, Colonel! Isn't the first rule of an officer "Don't involve your men in unnecessary danger?" [*Quickly he steals, still on his knees, to the table downstage right.*]

COLONEL: Don't be impertinent. Where's the torch?

BRINDSLEY: Er . . . the pub was closed.

HAROLD: You didn't go to the pub in that time, surely? You couldn't have done.

BRINDSLEY: Of course I did.

MISS FURNIVAL: But it's five streets away, Mr. Miller.

BRINDSLEY: Needs must when the Devil drives, Miss Furnival. Whatever that means. [*Quickly he lifts the table, and steals out of the room with it and the wrecked lamp.*]

COLONEL: [*who thinks he is still kneeling at his feet*]: Now look here: there's somethin' very peculiar goin' on in this room. I may not know about art, Miller, but I know men. I know a liar in the light, and I know one in the dark.

CAROL: Daddy!

COLONEL: I don't want to doubt your word, sir. All the same, I'd like your oath you went out to that public house. *Well?*

CAROL [*realizing he isn't there, raising her voice*]: Brin, Daddy's talking to you!

83 COLONEL: What are you shoutin' for?

BRINDSLEY [*rushing back from* HAROLD'*s room, still entangled in the lamp*]: Of course! I know! He's absolutely right. I was—just thinking it over for a moment.

COLONEL: Well? What's your answer?

BRINDSLEY: I . . . I couldn't agree with you more, sir.

COLONEL: What?

84   BRINDSLEY: That was a very perceptive remark you made there. Not everyone would have thought of that. Individual. You know. Almost witty. Well, it *was* witty. Why be ungenerous? . . .

COLONEL: Look, young man, are you trying to be funny?

BRINDSLEY [*ingratiatingly*]: Well, I'll try anything once . . .

HAROLD: I say, this is becoming a bit unpleasant, isn't it?

CAROL: It's becoming drearypegs.

COLONEL: Quiet, Dumpling. Let me handle this.

BRINDSLEY: What's there to handle, sir?

COLONEL: If you think I'm going to let my daughter marry a born liar, you're very much mistaken.

HAROLD: Marry!

CAROL: Well, that's the idea.

HAROLD: You and this young lady, Brin?

CAROL: Are what's laughingly known as engaged. Subject of course to Daddy's approval.

HAROLD: Well! [*Furious at the news, and at the fact that* BRINDSLEY *hasn't confided in him.*] What a surprise! . . .

BRINDSLEY: We were keeping it a secret.

HAROLD: Evidently. How long's this been going on, then?

BRINDSLEY: A few months.

85   HAROLD: You old slyboots.

BRINDSLEY [*nervous*]: I hope you approve, Harold.

HAROLD: Well, I must say, you know how to keep things to yourself.

BRINDSLEY [*placatingly*]: I meant to tell you, Harold . . . I really did. You were the one person I was going to tell.

HAROLD: Well, why didn't you, then?

BRINDSLEY: I don't know. I just never got around to it.

HAROLD: You saw me every day.

BRINDSLEY: I know.

HAROLD: You could have mentioned it at any time.

BRINDSLEY: I know.

HAROLD [*huffy*]: Well, it's your business. There's no obligation to share confidences. I've only been your neighbor for three years. I've always assumed there was more than a geographical closeness between us, but I was obviously mistaken.

BRINDSLEY: Oh, don't start getting huffy, Harold!

HAROLD: I'm not getting anything! I'm just saying it's surprising, that's all. Surprising and somewhat disappointing.

BRINDSLEY: Oh, look, Harold, please understand—

HAROLD [*shrill*]: There's no need to say anything! It'll just teach me in future not to bank too much on friendship. It's silly me again! Silly, stupid, trusting me!

[MISS FURNIVAL *rises in agitation and gropes her way to the drinks table.*]

COLONEL: Good God!

CAROL [*wheedling*]: Oh, come, Mr. Gorringe. We haven't told anybody. Not one single soulipegs. Really.

COLONEL: At the moment, Dumpling, there's nothing to tell. And I'm not sure there's going to be!

BRINDSLEY: Look, sir, we seem to have got off on the wrong foot. If it's my fault, I apologize.

MISS FURNIVAL [*groping about on the drinks table*]: My father always used to say, "To err is human: to forgive divine."

CAROL: I thought that was somebody else.

MISS FURNIVAL [*blithely*]: So many people copied him. [*She finds the open bottle of gin, lifts it and sniffs it eagerly.*]

CAROL: May I help you, Miss Furnival?

MISS FURNIVAL: No, thank you, Miss Melkett. I'm just getting myself another bitter lemon. That is—if I may, Mr. Miller?

BRINDSLEY: Of course. Help yourself.

MISS FURNIVAL: Thank you, most kind! [*She pours more gin into her glass and returns slowly to sit upstage on the edge of the rostrum.*]

COLONEL: Well, sir, wherever you are—

BRINDSLEY: Here, Colonel.

COLONEL: I'll overlook your damn peculiar behavior this once, but understand this, Miller. My daughter's dear to me. You show me you can look after her, and I'll consider the whole thing most favorably. I can't say fairer than that, can I?

BRINDSLEY: No, sir. Most fair, sir. Most fair. [*He pulls a hideous face one inch from the* COLONEL'*s.*]

CAROL: Of course he can look after me, Daddy. His works are going to be world famous. In five years I'll feel just like Mrs. Michelangelo.

HAROLD [*loftily*]: There wasn't a Mrs. Michelangelo, actually.

CAROL [*irritated*]: Wasn't there?

HAROLD: No. *He* had passionate feelings of a rather different nature.

CAROL: Really, Mr. Gorringe. I didn't know that. [*She puts out her tongue at him.*]

BRINDSLEY: Look, Harold, I'm sorry if I've hurt your feelings.

HAROLD [*loftily*]: You haven't.

BRINDSLEY: I know I have. Please forgive me.

80

CAROL: Oh do, Mr. Gorringe. Quarreling is so dreary. I hope we're all going to be great friends.

HAROLD: I'm not sure that I can contemplate a friendly relationship with a viper.

MISS FURNIVAL: Remember: to err is human, to forgive divine!

SCENE 5

COLONEL [*irritated*]: You just said that, madam.

[CLEA *enters, wearing dark glasses and carrying an air-bag. She stands in the doorway, amazed by the dark. She takes off her glasses, but this doesn't improve matters.*]

MISS FURNIVAL [*downing her gin happily*]: Did I?

CAROL: Brin's not really a viper. He's just artistic, aren't you, darling?

BRINDSLEY: Yes, darling.

[CAROL *sends him an audible kiss across the astonished* CLEA. *He returns it, equally audibly.*]

CAROL [*winningly*]: Come on, Mr. Gorringe. It really is a case of forgive and forgettipegs.

HAROLD: Is it reallypegs?

87 CAROL: Have another Ginette and lime. I'll have one with you. [*She rises and mixes the drink.*]

HAROLD [*rising*]: Oh, all right. I don't mind if I do.

CAROL: Let me mix it for you.

HAROLD: Ta. [*He crosses to her, narrowly missing* CLEA *who is now crossing*
88 *the room to the sofa, and gets his drink.*] I must say there's nothing nicer than having a booze-up with a pretty girl.

89 CAROL [*archly*]: You haven't seen me yet.

HAROLD: Oh, I just know it. Brindsley always had wonderful taste. I've often said to him, you've got the same taste in ladies as I have in porcelain. Ta.

[HAROLD *and* BRINDSLEY—*one from upstage, one from across the room— begin to converge on the sofa. On the word "modest" all three,* CLEA *in the middle, sit on it.* BRINDSLEY *of course imagines he is sitting next to* HAROLD.]

BRINDSLEY: Harold!

90 CAROL: Oh, don't be silly, Brin. Why be so modest? I found a photograph of one of his bits from two years ago, and I must say she was pretty stunning, in a blowsy sort of way.

HAROLD: Which one was that, then? I suppose she means Clea.

CAROL: Did you know her, Mr. Gorringe?

HAROLD: Oh yes. She's been around a long time.

[BRINDSLEY *nudges* CLEA *warningly—imagining she is* HAROLD. CLEA *gently bumps against* HAROLD.]

CAROL [*surprised*]: Has she?

HAROLD: Oh yes, dear. Or am I speaking out of turn?

BRINDSLEY: Not at all. I've told Carol all *about* Clea.

[*He bangs* CLEA *again, a little harder—who correspondingly bumps against* HAROLD.]

Though I must say, Harold, I'm surprised you call three months "a long time."

[CLEA *shoots him a look of total outrage at this lie.* HAROLD *is also astonished.*]

CAROL: What was she like?

BRINDSLEY [*meaningfully, into* CLEA'S *ear*]: I suppose you can hardly remember her, Harold.

HAROLD [*speaking across her*]: Why on earth shouldn't I?

BRINDSLEY: Well, since it was two years ago, you've probably forgotten.

HAROLD: Two years?!

BRINDSLEY: *Two years ago!*

91   [*He punches* CLEA *so hard that the rebound knocks* HAROLD *off the sofa, drink and all.*]

HAROLD [*picking himself up. Spitefully*]: Well, now since you mention it, I remember her perfectly. I mean, she's not one you can easily forget!

CAROL: Was she pretty?

HAROLD: No, not at all. In fact, I'd say the opposite. Actually she was rather plain.

BRINDSLEY: She wasn't!

HAROLD: I'm just giving my opinion.

BRINDSLEY: You've never given it before.

HAROLD [*leaning over* CLEA]: I was never *asked!* But since it's come up, I always thought she was ugly. For one thing, she had teeth like a picket fence—yellow and spiky. And for another, she had bad skin.

BRINDSLEY: She had nothing of the kind!

HAROLD: She did. I remember it perfectly. It was like a new pink wallpaper, with an old gray crumbly paper underneath.

MISS FURNIVAL: Quite right, Mr. Gorringe. I hardly ever saw her, but I do recall her skin. It was a strange color, as you say—and very coarse. . . . Not soft, as the skins of young ladies should be, if they *are* young ladies.

92   [CLEA *rises in outrage.*]

HAROLD: Aye, that's right. Coarse.

MISS FURNIVAL: And rather lumpy.

HAROLD: Very lumpy.

BRINDSLEY: This is disgraceful.

HAROLD: You knew I never liked her, Brindsley. She was too clever by half.

MISS FURNIVAL: And so tiresomely Bohemian.

CAROL: You mean she was as pretentious as her name?

[CLEA, *who has been reacting to this last exchange of comments about her like a spectator at a tennis match, now reacts to* CAROL *openmouthed.*]

I bet she was. That photograph I found showed her in a dirndl and a sort of sultry peasant blouse. She looked like *The Bartered Bride* done by Lloyds Bank.

[*They laugh,* BRINDSLEY *hardest of all. Guided by the noise,* CLEA *aims her hand and slaps his face.*]

BRINDSLEY: Ahh!

CAROL: What's wrong?

MISS FURNIVAL: What is it, Mr. Miller?

BRINDSLEY [*furiously*]: That's not very funny, Harold. What the hell's the matter with you?

93   [CLEA *makes her escape.*]

HAROLD [*indignant*]: With me?

BRINDSLEY: Well, I'm sure it wasn't the Colonel.

COLONEL: What wasn't, sir?

[BRINDSLEY, *groping about, catches* CLEA *by the bottom, and instantly recognizes it.*]

BRINDSLEY: *Clea!* . . .[*In horror.*] Clea!

[CLEA *breaks loose and moves away from him. During the following he tries to find her in the dark, and she narrowly avoids him.*]

COLONEL: What?

BRINDSLEY: I was just remembering her, sir. You're all talking the most awful nonsense. She was beautiful. . . . And anyway, Harold, you just said I was famous for my taste in women.

HAROLD: Aye, but it had its lapses.

BRINDSLEY [*frantically moving about*]: Rubbish! She was beautiful and tender and considerate and kind and loyal and witty and adorable in every way!

CAROL: You told me she was as cozy as a steel razor blade.

BRINDSLEY: Did I? Surely not! No. What I said was . . . something quite different . . . utterly different . . . entirely different . . . As different 94   as chalk from cheese. Although when you come to think of it, cheese isn't all that different from chalk! [*He gives his braying laugh.*]

COLONEL: Are you sure you know what you're talking about?

[*During this* CLEA *has reached the table, picked up a bottle of Scotch, and rejected it in favor of vodka, which she takes with her.*]

CAROL: You said to me in this room when I asked you what she was like, "She was a painter. Very honest. Very clever, and just about as cozy—"

95 BRINDSLEY [*stopping, exasperated*]: As a steel razor blade! Well then, I said it! So bloody what? . . .

CAROL: So nothing!

[~~He throws out his hands in a gesture of desperate exhaustion and bumps straight into CLEA. They instantly embrace, CLEA twining herself around him, her vodka bottle held aloft. A tiny pause.~~]

COLONEL: If that boy isn't touched, I don't know the meaning of the word!

~~CAROL: What's all this talk about her being kind and tender, all of a~~ sudden?

BRINDSLEY [*tenderly, holding* CLEA]: She could be. On occasion. Very.

CAROL: Very rare occasions, I imagine.

BRINDSLEY: Not so rare. [*He kisses* CLEA *again.*] Not so rare at all. [*He leads her softly past the irritated* CAROL, *toward the stairs.*]

CAROL: Meaning what, exactly? . . .[*Shouting.*] Brindsley, I'm talking to

96 you!!

BRINDSLEY [*sotto voce, into* CLEA's *ear as they stand just behind* HAROLD]: I can explain. Go up to the bedroom. Wait for me there.

HAROLD [*in amazement: thinking he is being addressed*]: Now? . . . Do you think this is quite the moment?

BRINDSLEY: Oh, God! . . . I wasn't talking to you!

~~CAROL: What did you say?~~

HAROLD [*to* CAROL]: I think he wants *you* upstairs. [*Slyly.*] For what purpose, I can't begin to imagine.

COLONEL: They're going to do some more of that plotting, I dare say.

MISS FURNIVAL: Lovers' talk, Colonel.

COLONEL: Very touching, I'm sure.

[BRINDSLEY *pushes* CLEA *ahead of him up the stairs.*]

MISS FURNIVAL: "Journeys end in lovers meeting," as my father always used to say.

COLONEL [*grimly*]: What a strikingly original father you seem to have had, madam!

[CAROL *joins the other two on the stairs. We see all three groping blindly up to the bedroom,* BRINDSLEY's *hands on* CLEA's *hips,* CAROL's *hands on* BRINDSLEY's *hips.*]

84

CAROL [*with a conspirator's stage whisper*]: What is it, darling? Has something gone wrong? What can't you move?
[*This next dialogue sotto voce on the stairs.*]
BRINDSLEY: Nothing. It's all back—every bit of it—except the sofa, and I've covered that up.
CAROL: You mean, we can have lights?
BRINDSLEY: Yes. . .NO!!
CAROL: Why not?
BRINDSLEY: Never mind!
CAROL: Why do you want me in the bedroom?
BRINDSLEY: I don't! Go away!
CAROL: Charming!
BRINDSLEY: I didn't mean that.
COLONEL: There you are. They *are* plotting again. [*Calling up.*] What the hell is going on up there?
BRINDSLEY: Nothing, Colonel. I've just remembered—there may be a torch under my bed. I keep it to blind the burglars with. Have another drink, Colonel!

97 [*He pushes CLEA into the bedroom and shuts the door.*]
COLONEL: What d'you mean another? I haven't had *one* yet!
MISS FURNIVAL: Oh! Poor Colonel! Let me get you one.
98 COLONEL [*rising*]: I can get one for myself, thank you. Let me get you another lemonade.
MISS FURNIVAL [*rising*]: No, thank you, Colonel, I'll manage myself. It's good practice!
[*They grope toward the drinks table. Above, CLEA and BRINDSLEY sit on the bed.*]
CLEA: So this is what they mean by a blind date! What the hell is going on?
BRINDSLEY [*sarcastic*]: Nothing! Georg Bamberger is only coming to see my work tonight, and we've got a main fuse.
CLEA: Is that the reason for all this furtive clutching?
BRINDSLEY: Look, I can't explain things at the moment.
CLEA: Who's that—[*debutante accent*] "frightful gel"?
BRINDSLEY: Just a friend.
CLEA: She sounded more than that.
BRINDSLEY: Well, if you must know, it's Carol. I've told you about her.
CLEA: The Idiot Deb?
BRINDSLEY: She's a very sweet girl. As a matter of fact we've become very good friends in the last six weeks.

CLEA: How good?

BRINDSLEY: Just good.

CLEA: And have you become friends with her father too?

BRINDSLEY: If it's any of your business, they just dropped in to meet Mr. Bamberger.

CLEA: What was it you wanted to tell me on the phone tonight?

BRINDSLEY: Nothing.

CLEA: You're lying!

BRINDSLEY: Look, Clea, if you ever loved me, just slip away quietly with no more questions, and I'll come round later and explain everything, I promise.

CLEA: I don't believe you.

BRINDSLEY: Please, darling . . . please . . . please . . . please!

[They kiss, passionately, stretched out on the bed.]

COLONEL [*pouring*]: At last . . . a decent glass of Scotch. Are you getting your lemonade?

MISS FURNIVAL [*cheerfully pouring herself an enormous gin*]: Oh yes, thank you, Colonel!

COLONEL: I'm just wonderin' if this Bamberger fellow is goin' to show up at all. He's half an hour late already.

HAROLD: Oh! That's nothing, Colonel. Millionaires are always late. It's their thing.

MISS FURNIVAL: I'm sure you're right, Mr. Gorringe. That's how *I* imagine them. Hands like silk, and always two hours late.

CAROL: Brin's been up there a long time. What can he be doing?

HAROLD: Maybe he's got that Clea hidden away in his bedroom, and they're having a tête-à-tête!!

CAROL: What a fragrant suggestion, Mr. Gorringe.

BRINDSLEY [*disengaging himself*]: No one in the world kisses like you.

CLEA: I missed you so badly, Brin. I had to see you. I've thought about nothing else these past six weeks. Brin, I made the most awful mistake walking out.

BRINDSLEY: Clea—*please!*

CLEA: I mean we've known each other for four years. We can't just throw each other away like old newspapers.

BRINDSLEY: I don't see why not. You know my politics, you've heard my gossip, and you've certainly been through all my entertainment section.

CLEA: Well, how about a second edition?

BRINDSLEY: Darling, we simply can't talk about this now. Can't you trust me just for an hour?

CLEA: Of course I can, darling. You don't want me down there?
BRINDSLEY: No.
CLEA: Then I'll get undressed and go quietly to bed. When you've got rid of them all, I'll be waiting.
BRINDSLEY: That's a terrible idea!
CLEA [*reaching for him*]: I think it's lovely. A little happy relaxation for us both.
BRINDSLEY [*falling off the bed*]: I'm perfectly relaxed!
CAROL: Brindsley!
CLEA: "Too solemn for day, too sweet for night. Come not in darkness, come not in light." That's me, isn't it?
BRINDSLEY: Of course not. I just can't explain now, that's all.
CLEA: Oh, very well, you can explain later . . . in bed!
BRINDSLEY: Not tonight, Clea.
CLEA: Either that or I come down and discover your sordid secret.
BRINDSLEY: There *is* no sordid secret!
~~CLEA: Then you won't mind my coming down.~~
CAROL, COLONEL [*roaring together*]: BRINDSLEY!!!
BRINDSLEY: ~~Oh, God!! . . . All right, stay. Only keep quiet. Black-~~
100 ~~mailing bitch!~~ [*He emerges at the top of the stairs.*] Yes, my sweet?
CAROL: What are you doing up there? You've been an eternity!
BRINDSLEY: I . . . I . . . I'm just looking in the bathroom, my darling. You never know what you might find in that clever little cabinet!
COLONEL [*moving to the stairs*]: Are you trying to madden me, sir? Are you trying to put me in a fury?
BRINDSLEY: Certainly not, sir!
COLONEL: I warn you, Miller, it's not difficult! In the old days in the regiment I was known for my furies! I was famous for my furies! . . . Do you hear?
101 CLEA: I may sing! [~~She goes off into the bathroom.~~]
BRINDSLEY: I may knock your teeth in!
COLONEL: What did you say?
CAROL: Brin! How dare you talk to Daddy like that!
102 BRINDSLEY: Oh!! I . . . I . . . I wasn't talking to Daddy like that . . .
CAROL: Then who *were* you talking to?
BRINDSLEY: I was talking to no one! Myself I was talking to! I was saying . . . "If I keep groping about up here like this, I might knock my teeth in!"
COLONEL: Mad! . . . Mad! . . . Mad as the south wind! It's the only explanation—you've got yourself engaged to a lunatic.

CAROL: There's something going on up there, and I'm coming up to find
out what it is. Do you hear me, Brin?

BRINDSLEY: Carol—no!

CAROL [*climbing the stairs*]: I'm not such a fool as you take me for. I know

103   when you're hiding something. Your voice goes all deceitful—very,
very foxipegs!

BRINDSLEY: Darling, please. That's not very ladylike . . . I'm sure the

SCENE 6   Colonel won't approve of you entering a man's bedroom in the dark!

[*Enter* SCHUPPANZIGH. *He wears the overcoat and peaked cap of the London*

104   *Electricity Board and carries a large toolbag, similarly labeled.*]

CAROL: I'm comin' up, Brindsley, I'm comin' up!!!

BRINDSLEY [*scrambling down*]: I'm coming down . . . . We'll all have a
nice cozy drink . . .

SCHUPPANZIGH [*German accent*]: 'Allo, please? Mr. Miller? Mr. Miller?
I've come as was arranged.

BRINDSLEY: My God . . . it's Bamberger!

CAROL: Bamberger?

105   BRINDSLEY: Yes, Bamberger. [~~BRINDSLEY rushes down the remaining stairs,~~
~~pulling Carol with him.~~]

SCHUPPANZIGH: You must have thought I was never coming! [*He takes
off his overcoat and cap.*]

BRINDSLEY: Not at all. I'm delighted you could spare the time. I know
how busy you are. I'm afraid we've had the most idiotic disaster. We've
had a fuse.

HAROLD: You'll have to speak up, dear, he's stone deaf!

BRINDSLEY [*yelling*]: We've had a fuse—not the best conditions for seeing
sculpture.

SCHUPPANZIGH: Please not to worry. Here!

[*He produces a torch from his pocket and "lights" it. The light on stage*
dims a little, as usual, to indicate this. All relax with audible sighs of

106   *pleasure.* SCHUPPANZIGH *at once places his toolbag on the Regency chair,*
and puts his coat and cap on top of it, concealing the fact that it is one of
HAROLD's *chairs.*]

CAROL: Oh, what a relief!

107   BRINDSLEY [*hastily dragging the sheet over the rest of the sofa*]: Do you always
travel with a torch?

SCHUPPANZIGH: Mostly, yes. It helps to see details. [*Seeing the others.*]
You are holding a private view?

MISS FURNIVAL: Oh no! I was just going, I'd hate to distract you.

SCHUPPANZIGH: Please not on my account, dear lady, I am not so easily
distracted.

MISS FURNIVAL [*charmed*]: Oh! . . .

BRINDSLEY [*yelling in his ear*]: May I present Colonel Melkett?

COLONEL [*yelling in his other ear*]: A great honor, sir!

SCHUPPANZIGH [*banging his ear, to clear it*]: No, no, mine—mine!

BRINDSLEY: Miss Carol Melkett!

108   CAROL [*screeching in his ear*]: I say: hello. So glad you got here! It's terribly
kind of you to take such an interest!

SCHUPPANZIGH: Not at all. *Vous êtes très gentil.*

CAROL [*yelling*]: What would you like to drink?

SCHUPPANZIGH [*bewildered*]: A little vodka would be beautiful!

CAROL: Of course!

BRINDSLEY: Harold Gorringe—a neighbor of mine!

HAROLD [*shouting*]: How do? Very honored, I'm sure.

SCHUPPANZIGH: Enchanted.

HAROLD: I must say it's a real thrill, meeting you!

109   BRINDSLEY: And another neighbor, Miss Furnival!

SCHUPPANZIGH: Enchanted.

MISS FURNIVAL [*hooting in his ear*]: I'm afraid we've all been taking refuge
from the *storm*, as it were. [*Exclaiming as she holds* SCHUPPANZIGH'*s
hand.*] Oh! It *is* true! They *are* softer! Much, much softer!

SCHUPPANZIGH [*utterly confused as she strokes his hand*]: Softer? Please?

[BRINDSLEY *and* HAROLD *pull her away, and she subsides onto the sofa.*]

BRINDSLEY: Miss Furnival, please!

CAROL [*at the drinks table*]: Darling, where's the vodka?

BRINDSLEY: It's on the table.

CAROL: No, it isn't.

BRINDSLEY: It must be!

[~~Above,~~ ~~CLEA~~ ~~reenters~~ ~~wearing~~ ~~the~~ ~~top~~ ~~half~~ ~~of~~ ~~BRINDSLEY's~~ ~~pajamas~~ ~~and~~
~~nothing~~ ~~else.~~ ~~She~~ ~~gets~~ ~~into~~ ~~bed,~~ ~~still~~ ~~clutching~~ ~~the~~ ~~vodka~~ ~~bottle~~ ~~and~~ ~~carrying~~
~~a~~ ~~plastic~~ ~~toothmug.~~]

CAROL: Well, see for yourself. There's Winnie and Ginette, and Vera has
quite vanished, the naughty girl!

BRINDSLEY: She can't have done.

SCHUPPANZIGH: Please don't concern yourselves. I am pressed for time.
If I might just be shown where to go.

BRINDSLEY: Of course. It's through the studio there. Darling, if you would
just show our guest into the studio—*with his torch.*

CAROL: What?? . . .

BRINDSLEY [*sotto voce*]: *The sofa!* . . .Get him out of here!

CAROL: Oh yes!! . . .

110 SCHUPPANZIGH [*sighting the sculpture*]: Oh! Good gracious! What an extraordinary object!

BRINDSLEY: Oh, that's just a spare piece of my work I keep in here!

SCHUPPANZIGH: Spare, maybe, but fascinating!

BRINDSLEY: You really think so?

SCHUPPANZIGH [*approaching it*]: I do! *Ja!*

BRINDSLEY: Well, in that case you should see my main collection. It's next door. My fiancée will show you!

[MISS FURNIVAL *sits on the sofa. She is now quite drunk.*]

SCHUPPANZIGH: One amazement at a time, if you please! In this gluttonous age it is easy to get visual indigestion—hard to find visual Alka Seltzer. . . . Permit me to digest this first!

BRINDSLEY: Oh, by all means. . . . Good, yes. . . . There's no hurry— no hurry at all . . . . Only . . . [*inspired*], why don't you digest it *in the dark?*

SCHUPPANZIGH: I beg your pardon?

BRINDSLEY: You'll never believe it, sir, but I actually made that piece to be appreciated in the dark. I was working on a very interesting theory. You know how the Victorians said, "Children should be seen and not heard"? Well, I say, "Art should be felt and not seen."

SCHUPPANZIGH: Amazing.

BRINDSLEY: Yes, isn't it. I call it my theory of Factual Tactility. If it doesn't stab you to the quick—it's not art. Look! Why don't you give me that torch, and try for yourself?

SCHUPPANZIGH: Very well, I will! [*He hands* BRINDSLEY *the torch.*]

BRINDSLEY: Thank you!

[*He turns off the torch and hands it to* CAROL. *At the same moment* MISS FURNIVAL *quietly lies down, her full length on the sofa.*]

Now just stretch out your arms and feel it all over, sir. [*He steals toward the studio.*] Have a good long feel!

[SCHUPPANZIGH *embraces the metal sculpture with a fervent clash. He pulls at the two metal prongs.*]

Do you see what I mean? [*Silently he opens the curtains.*]

SCHUPPANZIGH: Amazing! . . . Absolutely incredible! . . . It's quite true . . . Like this, the piece becomes a masterpiece at once.

BRINDSLEY [*astonished*]: It does?

SCHUPPANZIGH: But of course! I feel it here—and here—the two needles of man's unrest! . . .Self-love and self-hate, leading to the same point! That's the meaning of the work, isn't it?

BRINDSLEY: Of course. You've got it in one! You're obviously a great expert, sir!

[*Quietly he pulls the sofa into the studio, bearing on it the supine* MISS FURNIVAL, *who vaguely waves goodbye as she disappears.*]

SCHUPPANZIGH: Not at all. *Vous êtes très gentil*—but it is evident! . . .Standing here in the dark, one can feel the vital thrust of the argument! The essential anguish! The stress and the torment of our times! It is simple but not simpleminded! Ingenious, but not ingenuous! Above all, it has real moral force! Of how many modern works can one say that, good people?

CAROL [*gushing*]: Oh, none, none at all really!

SCHUPPANZIGH: I hope I do not lecture. It can be a fault with me.

CAROL: Not at all! I could listen all night, it's so profound.

HAROLD: Me too. Really deep!

COLONEL: I don't know anything about this myself, sir, but it's an honor to listen to you.

[*He starts off upstage in search of the sofa, seating himself tentatively in the air, then moving himself along in a sitting position, trying to find it with his rear end. At the same moment* BRINDSLEY *emerges from the studio, closes the curtains behind him, and gropes his way to the upstage corner where there stands a small packing case. This he carries forward, hopefully to do duty for the missing sofa. Just as he places it on the ground the traveling* COLONEL *sits on it, trapping* BRINDSLEY'S *hand beneath his weight. During the following,* BRINDSLEY *tries frantically to free himself.*]

SCHUPPANZIGH: *Vous êtes très gentil!*

HAROLD: You mean to say you see all that in a bit of metal?

SCHUPPANZIGH: A *tiny* bit of metal, that's the point. A miracle of compression. You want my opinion, this boy is a genius. A master of the miniature. In the space of a matchbox he can realize anything he wants—the black virginity of Chartres! The white chorale of the Acropolis! *Wunderbar!*

CAROL: Oh, how super!

SCHUPPANZIGH: You should charge immense sums for work like this, Mr. Miller. They should be very, very expensive! This one, for example, how much is this?

BRINDSLEY: Fifty—

CAROL: Five hundred guineas!

SCHUPPANZIGH: Ah so! Very cheap.

HAROLD: Cheap!

CAROL: I think so, Mr. Gorringe. Well . . . so will you have it, then?

SCHUPPANZIGH: Me?

BRINDSLEY: Darling . . . aren't you rushing things just a little? Perhaps you would like to see the rest of my work.

SCHUPPANZIGH: Alas, I have no more time. To linger would be pleasant, but alas, I must work . . . Also, as Moses discovered, it is sufficient to *glimpse* milk and honey. One does not have to wolf them down!

BRINDSLEY: Well.

COLONEL: Well . . .

HAROLD: Well . . .

CAROL: Well . . . would you like it then?

SCHUPPANZIGH: Very much.

111   COLONEL [*rising.* BRINDSLEY *is freed at last*]: For five hundred guineas?

SCHUPPANZIGH: Certainly—if I had it!

HAROLD: According to the Sunday paper, you must be worth at least seventeen million pounds.

SCHUPPANZIGH: The Sunday papers are notoriously ill-informed. According to my last bank statement, I was worth one hundred pounds, eight shillings, and fourpence.

HAROLD: You mean you've gone broke?

SCHUPPANZIGH: No. I mean I never had any more.

COLONEL: Now look, sir, I know millionaires are supposed to be eccentric, but this is gettin' tiresome.

CAROL: Daddy, ssh!

SCHUPPANZIGH: Millionaires? Who do you think I am?

COLONEL: Dammit, man! You must know who you are!

CAROL: Mr. Bamberger, is this some kind of joke you like to play?

SCHUPPANZIGH: Excuse me. That is not my name.

BRINDSLEY: It isn't?

SCHUPPANZIGH: No. My name is Schuppanzigh. Franz Schuppanzigh. Born in Weimar, 1905. Student of philosophy at Heidelberg, 1934. Refugee to this country, 1938. Regular employment ever since with the London Electricity Board!

112   [*All rise.*]

CAROL: Electricity?

MISS FURNIVAL: Electricity!

BRINDSLEY: You mean you're not—?

HAROLD: Of course he's not!

SCHUPPANZIGH: But who did you imagine I was?

HAROLD [*furious*]: How dare you? [*He snatches the electrician's torch.*]

SCHUPPANZIGH [*retreating before him*]: Please?

HAROLD: Of all the nerve, coming in here, giving us a lecture about needles and virgins, and all the time you're simply here to mend the fuses!

COLONEL: I agree with you, sir. It's monstrous!

SCHUPPANZIGH [*bewildered*]: It is?

[*The* COLONEL *takes the torch and shines it pitilessly in the man's face.*]

COLONEL: You come in here, a public servant, and proceed to harangue your employers, unasked and uninvited.

SCHUPPANZIGH [*bewildered*]: Excuse me. But I *was* invited.

COLONEL: Don't answer back. In my day you would have been fired on the spot for impertinence.

CAROL: Daddy's absolutely right! Ever since the Beatles, the lower classes think they can behave exactly as they want.

COLONEL [*handing the torch to* BRINDSLEY]: Miller, will you kindly show this feller his work?

BRINDSLEY: The mains are in the cellar. There's a trapdoor. [*Indicating.*] Do you mind?

113 SCHUPPANZIGH [*snatching the torch furiously*]: Why should I mind? It's why I came, after all! [*He takes his coat, cap, and bag off* HAROLD'*s Regency chair . . . seeing it*] Now there is a really beautiful chair!

[BRINDSLEY *stares at the chair aghast—and in a twinkling seats himself in it to conceal it.*]

BRINDSLEY [*exasperated*]: Why don't you just go into the cellar?

SCHUPPANZIGH: How? Where is it?

~~BRINDSLEY [to CAROL]: Darling, will you open the trap, please.~~

CAROL: Me? [*Understanding—as he indicates the chair*] Oh—yes! [*She kneels and struggles to open the trap.*]

COLONEL [*to* BRINDSLEY]: Well, I must say, that's very gallant of you, Miller.

BRINDSLEY: I've got a sudden touch of lumbago, sir. It often afflicts me after long spells in the dark.

CAROL [*very sympathetic*]: Oh, darling! Has it come back?

BRINDSLEY: I'm afraid it has, my sweet.

HAROLD [*opening the trap*]: Here, let me. I'm not as frail as our wilting ~~friend. [To SCHUPPANZIGH.] Well, down you go,~~ you!

114 SCHUPPANZIGH [*shrugging*]: So. Farewell. I leave the light of Art for the dark of Science.

HAROLD: Let's have a little less of your lip, shall we?

SCHUPPANZIGH: Excuse me.

SCENE 7

[SCHUPPANZIGH *descends through the trap, taking the torch with him.* HAROLD *slams the trapdoor down irritably after him, and of course the lights immediately come up full. There is a long pause. All stand about embarrassed. Suddenly they hear the noise of* MISS FURNIVAL *singing "~~Rock of Ages~~" in a high drunken voice from behind the curtain. Above, attracted by the noise of the slam,* CLEA ~~gets out of bed, still clutching the vodka and toothmug, opens the door, and~~ stands at the top of the stairs listening.]*

BRINDSLEY: None of this evening is happening.

CAROL: Cheer up, darling. In a few minutes everything will be all right. Mr. Bamberger will arrive in the light—he'll adore your work and give you twenty thousand pounds for your whole collection.

BRINDSLEY [*sarcastic*]: Oh, yes!

CAROL: Then we can buy a super Georgian house and live what's laughingly known as happily ever after. I want to leave this place just as soon as we're married.

[CLEA *hears this. Her mouth opens wide.*]

BRINDSLEY [*nervously*]: Sssh!

CAROL: Why? I don't want to live in a slum for our first couple of years— like other newlyweds.

BRINDSLEY: Sssh! Ssssh! . . .

CAROL: What's the matter with you?

BRINDSLEY: The gods listen, darling. They've given me a terrible night so far. They may do worse.

CAROL [*cooing*]: I know, darling. You've had a filthy evening. Poor babykins. But I'll fight them with you. I don't care a fig for those naughty old Goddipegs! [*Looking up.*] Do you hear? Not a single little fig!

[CLEA *aims at the voice and sends a jet of vodka splashing down over* CAROL.]

Ahh!!!

BRINDSLEY: What is it?

CAROL: It's raining!

BRINDSLEY: Don't be ridiculous.

CAROL: I'm all wet!

BRINDSLEY: How can you be?

[CLEA *throws vodka over a wider area.* HAROLD *gets it.*]

HAROLD: Hey, what's going on?

BRINDSLEY: What?

COLONEL: What the devil's the matter with you all? What are you hollerin' for? [*He gets a slug of vodka in the face.*] Ahh!!

BRINDSLEY [*inspired*]: It's a leak—the water mains must have gone now!

HAROLD: Oh, good God!

BRINDSLEY: It must be!

[*Mischievously,* CLEA *raps her bottle loudly on the top stair. There is a terrified silence. All look up.*]

HAROLD: Don't say there's someone else here.

BRINDSLEY: Good Lord!

COLONEL: Who's there?

[*Silence from above.*]

Come on! I know you're there!

BRINDSLEY [*improvising wildly*]: I—I bet you it's Mrs. Punnet.

[CLEA *looks astonished.*]

COLONEL: Who?

BRINDSLEY [*for* CLEA'*s benefit*]: Mrs. Punnet. My cleaning woman.

HAROLD: Cleaning woman?

BRINDSLEY: She does for me on Mondays, Wednesdays, and Fridays.

CAROL: Well, what would she be doing here now?

BRINDSLEY: I've just remembered—she rang up and said she'd look in about six to tidy up the place.

COLONEL: Dammit, man, it's almost eleven.

HAROLD: She's not that conscientious. She couldn't be!

CAROL: Not these days!

COLONEL: Well, we'll soon see. [*Calling up.*] Mrs. Punnet?

BRINDSLEY [*desperately*]: Don't interrupt her, sir. She doesn't like to be disturbed when she's working. Why don't we just leave her to potter around upstairs with her duster?

COLONEL: Let us first just see if it's her. Is that you, Mrs. Punnet? . . .

[CLEA *keeps still.*]

COLONEL [*roaring*]: MRS. PUNNET!

CLEA [*deciding on a cockney voice of great antiquity*]: 'Allo! Yes?

BRINDSLEY [*weakly*]: It is. Good heavens, Mrs. Punnet, what on earth are you doing up there?

CLEA: I'm just giving your bedroom a bit of a tidy, sir.

BRINDSLEY: At this time of night?

[*The mischief in* CLEA *begins to take over.*]

CLEA: Better late than never, sir, as they say. I know how you like your bedroom to be nice and inviting when you're giving one of your parties.

BRINDSLEY: Yes, yes, yes, of course . . .

CAROL: When did you come, madam?

CLEA: Just a few minutes ago, sir. I didn't like to disturb you, so I come on up 'ere.

HAROLD: Was it you pouring all that water on us, then?

CLEA: Water? Good 'eavens, I must have upset something. It's as black as Newgate's Knocker up 'ere. Are you playing one of your saucy games, Mr. Miller?

BRINDSLEY: No, Mrs. Punnet. We've had a fuse. It's all over the house.

CLEA: Oh! A *fuse!* I thought it might be one of them saucy games in the dark, sir: Sardines or Piccadilly. The kind that end in a general squeeze-up. I know you're rather partial to kinky games, Mr. Miller, so I just wondered. [*She starts to come down the stairs.*]

BRINDSLEY [*distinctly*]: It is a fuse, Mrs. Punnet. The man's mending it now. The lights will be on *any minute!*

CLEA: Well, that'll be a relief for you, won't it? [*She dashes the vodka accurately in his face, passes him by, and comes into the room.*]

BRINDSLEY: Yes, of course. Now why don't you just go on home?

CLEA: I'm sorry I couldn't come before, sir. I was delayed, you see. My Rosie's been taken queer again.

BRINDSLEY: I quite understand! [*He gropes around trying to hide her, but she continuously evades him.*]

CLEA [*relentlessly*]: It's her tummy. There's a lump under her belly button the size of a grapefruit.

HAROLD: Oh, how nasty!

CLEA: Horrid. Poor little Rosie. I said to her this evening, I said, "There's no good your being mulish, my girl. You're going to the hospital first thing tomorrow morning and getting yourself ultraviolated!"

BRINDSLEY: Well, hadn't you better be getting back to poor little Rosie? She must need you, surely? And there's really nothing you can do here tonight.

CLEA [*meaningfully*]: Are you sure of that, sir?

BRINDSLEY: Positive, thank you.

[*They are close now.*]

CLEA: I mean, I know what this place can be like after one of your evenings. A gypsy caravan isn't in it. Gin bottles all over the floor! Bras and panties in the sink! And God knows what in the—

[BRINDSLEY *muzzles her with his hand. She bites it hard, and he drops to his knees in silent agony.*]

COLONEL: Please watch what you say, madam. You don't know it, but you're in the presence of Mr. Miller's fiancée.

CLEA: Fiancée?

COLONEL: Yes, and I am her father.

CLEA: Well, I never! . . . Oh, Mr. Miller! I'm so 'appy for you! . . . Fiancée! Oh, sir! And you never *told* me!

BRINDSLEY: I was keeping it a surprise.

CLEA: Well, I never! Oh, how lovely! . . . May I kiss you, sir, please?

BRINDSLEY [*on his knees*]: Well, yes, yes, of course . . .

[CLEA *gropes for his ear, finds it, and twists it.*]

CLEA: Oh, sir, I'm so pleased for you! And for *you*, miss, too!

CAROL: Thank you.

CLEA [*to* COLONEL MELKETT]: And for *you*, sir.

COLONEL: Thank you.

CLEA: You must be Miss Clea's father.

COLONEL: Miss Clea? I don't understand.

[*Triumphantly she sticks out her tongue at* BRINDSLEY, *who collapses his length on the floor, face·down, in a gesture of total surrender. For him it is the end. The evening can hold no further disasters for him.*]

CLEA [*to* CAROL]: Well, I never! So you've got him at last! Well done, Miss Clea! I never thought you would—not after four years . . .

BRINDSLEY: No—no—no—no . . .

CLEA: Forgive me, sir, if I'm speaking out of turn, but you must admit four years is a long time to be courting one woman. Four days is stretching it a bit nowadays!

BRINDSLEY [*weakly*]: Mrs. Punnet, *please!*

CAROL: Four years!

CLEA: Well, yes, dear. It's been all of that and a bit more really, hasn't it? [*In a stage whisper.*] And of course it's just in time. It was getting a bit prominent, your little bun in the oven.

[CAROL *screeches with disgust.* BRINDSLEY *covers his ears.*]

Oh, miss, I don't mean that's why he popped the question. Of course it's not. He's always been stuck on you. He told me so, not one week ago, in this room. [*Sentimentally.*] "Mrs. Punnet," he says, "Mrs. Punnet, as far as I'm concerned you can keep the rest of them—Miss Clea will always be on top of the heap for me." "Oh," I says, "then what about that debutante bit, Carol, the one you're always telling me about?" "Oh, 'er," he says, "she's just a bit of Knightsbridge candyfloss. A couple of licks and you've 'ad 'er."

[*There is a long pause.* CLEA *is now sitting on the table, swinging her vodka bottle in absolute command of the situation.*]

COLONEL [*faintly; at last grappling with the situation*]: Did you say four years, madam?

CLEA [*in her own voice, quiet*]: Yes, Colonel. Four years, in this room.

HAROLD: I know that voice. It's Clea!

MISS FURNIVAL [*surprised*]: Clea!

CAROL [*horrified*]: Clea!

BRINDSLEY [*unconvincingly*]: Clea!

CLEA: Surprised, Brin?

118 CAROL [*understanding*]: Clea! . . .

COLONEL: I don't understand anything that's going on in this room!

CLEA: I know. It is a very odd room, isn't it? It's like a magic dark room, where everything happens the wrong way round. Rain falls indoors, the daily comes at night, and turns in a second from a nice maid into nasty mistress.

BRINDSLEY: Be quiet, Clea!

CLEA: At last! One real word of protest! Have you finished lying, then? Have you eaten the last crumb of humble pie? Oh, you coward, you bloody coward! Just because you didn't want to marry me, did you have to settle for this lot?

CAROL: Marry!

COLONEL: Marry?

CLEA: Four years of meaning to end in this triviality! Miss Laughingly-Known-As and her Daddipegs!

119 CAROL: Stop her! She's disgusting!

COLONEL: How can I, for God's sake?

CAROL: Well, where's all that bloody resource you keep talking about?

[*The* COLONEL *goes to her but takes* CLEA'*s hand by mistake.*]

COLONEL: Now calm down, Dumpling. Keep your head. . . . There— hold my hand, that's it, now Daddy's here. Everything is under control. All right?

CLEA: Are you sure that is your daughter's hand you're holding, Colonel?

COLONEL: What? Carol, isn't this your hand?

CAROL: No.

CLEA: You must have lived with your daughter for well over twenty years, Colonel. What remarkable use you've made of your eyes.

120 [*There is another pause. The* COLONEL *moves away in embarrassment.*]

CLEA [*wickedly*]: All right! Kinky game time! . . . Let's all play Guess the Hand.

HAROLD: Oh, good God!

CLEA: Or would you rather Guess the Lips, Harold?

CAROL: How disgusting!

CLEA: Well, that's me, dear. [CAROL'*s accent.*] I'm Queen Disgustipegs!

[*She seizes* CAROL'*s hand and puts it into* HAROLD'*s.*] Who's that?

CAROL: I don't know.

CLEA: Guess.

CAROL: I don't know, and I don't care.

CLEA: Oh, go on. Have a go!

CAROL: It's Brin, of course: You can't trick me like that! It's Brindsley's stupid hand.

HAROLD: I'm afraid you're wrong. It's me.

CAROL [*struggling*]: It's not. You're lying.

HAROLD [*holding on*]: I'm not. I don't lie.

CAROL: You're lying! . . .You're lying!

HAROLD: I'm not.

121   [CAROL breaks away ~~and blunders upstage~~. She is becoming hysterical.]

CLEA: You try it, Harold. Take the hand on your right.

HAROLD: I'm not playing. It's a bloody silly game.

CLEA: Go on . . .[*She seizes his hand and puts it into* BRINDSLEY's.] Well?

HAROLD: It's Brin.

BRINDSLEY: Yes.

CLEA: Well done! [*She sits on the low stool.*]

CAROL [*outraged*]: How does he know that? How does *he* know your hand and I don't?

BRINDSLEY: Calm down, Carol.

CAROL: Answer me! I want to know!

BRINDSLEY: Stop it!

CAROL: I won't!

BRINDSLEY: You're getting hysterical!

CAROL: Leave me alone! I want to go home.

122   [And suddenly MISS FURNIVAL gives a sharp short scream ~~and blunders out through the curtains.~~]

MISS FURNIVAL: Prams! Prams! Prams—in the supermarket! . . .

[*They all freeze. She is evidently out of control in a world of her own fears. She speaks quickly and strangely.*]

All those hideous wire prams full of babies and bottles—"Cornflakes over there" is all they say—and then they leave you to yourself. Biscuits over there—cat food over there—fish cakes over there—Airwick over there! Pink stamps, green stamps, free balloons—television dinners— pay as you go out—oh, Daddy, it's *awful!* . . . And then the godless ones, the heathens in their leather jackets—laughing me to scorn! But not for long. Oh, no! Who shall stand when He appeareth? He'll strike them from their motorcycles! He'll dash their helmets to the ground! Yes, verily, I say unto thee—there shall be an end of gasoline! An end to cigarette puffing and jostling with hips. . . . Keep off . . . Keep off! Keep off! . . .[*She runs drunkenly across the room and collides with* HAROLD.]

HAROLD: Come on, Ferny, I think it's time we went home.

MISS FURNIVAL [*pulling herself together*]: Yes. You're quite right. . . .[*With an attempt at grandeur.*] I'm sorry I can't stay any longer, Mr. Miller; but your millionaire is unpardonably late. So typical of modern manners. . . . Express my regrets, if you please.

BRINDSLEY: Certainly.

[*Leaning heavily on* HAROLD's *arm she leaves the room. He shuts the door after them.*]

SCENE 8

Thank you, Clea. Thank you very much.

CLEA: Any time.

BRINDSLEY: You had no right.

CLEA: No?

BRINDSLEY: *You* walked out on *me*. [*He joins her on the low stool.*]

CLEA: Is that what I did?

BRINDSLEY: You said you never wanted to see me again.

CLEA: I never saw you at all—how could you be walked out on? You should *live* in the dark, Brindsley. It's your natural element.

BRINDSLEY: Whatever that means.

CLEA: It means you don't really want to be seen. Why is that, Brindsley? Do you think if someone really saw you, they would never love you?

BRINDSLEY: Oh, go away.

123

CLEA: I want to know.

BRINDSLEY: Yes, you always want to know. Pick-pick-pick away! Why is *that*, Clea? Have you ever thought why you need to do it? Well?

CLEA: Perhaps because I care about you.

BRINDSLEY: Perhaps there's nothing to care about. Just a fake artist.

CLEA: Stop pitying yourself. It's always your vice. I told you when I met you: you could either be a good artist, or a chic fake. You didn't like it, because I refused just to give you applause.

BRINDSLEY: God knows, you certainly did that!

CLEA: Is that what *she* gives you? Twenty hours of ego-massage every day?

BRINDSLEY: At least our life together isn't the replica of the Holy Inquisition you made of ours. I didn't have an affair with you: it was just four years of nooky with Torquemada!

CLEA: And don't say you didn't enjoy it!

BRINDSLEY: Enjoy it? I hated every second of it.

CLEA: Yes, I remember.

BRINDSLEY: Every second!

CLEA: I recall.

BRINDSLEY: When you left for Finland, it was the happiest day of my life.

CLEA: Mine, too!

BRINDSLEY: I sighed with relief.

CLEA: So did I.

BRINDSLEY: I went out dancing that very night.

CLEA: So did I. It was out with the lyre and the timbrel.

BRINDSLEY: Good. Then that's all right.

CLEA: Fine.

BRINDSLEY: Super!

CLEA: Duper!

BRINDSLEY: It's lovely to see you looking so happy.

CLEA: You too. Radiant with self-fulfillment.

[A pause.]

BRINDSLEY: If you felt like this, why did you come back?

CLEA: If *you* felt like this, why did you tell Mrs. Punnet I was still at the top of the heap?

BRINDSLEY: I never said that!

CLEA: You did.

BRINDSLEY: Never!

CLEA: You *did!*

BRINDSLEY: Of course I didn't. You invented that ten minutes ago, when you were *playing* Mrs. Punnet.

CLEA: I—oh! So I did! . . .

[*They both giggle. She falls happily against his shoulder.*]

BRINDSLEY: You know something—I'm not sure she's not right.

[*During this exchange the* COLONEL *and* CAROL *have been standing frozen with astonished anger. Now the outraged father takes over. He is very angry.*]

124   COLONEL: No doubt this is very funny to you two.

CLEA: It is, quite, actually.

COLONEL: I'm not so easily amused, however, madam.

BRINDSLEY: Now look, Colonel—

COLONEL: Hold your tongue, sir, I'm talking. Do you know what would have happened to a young man in my day who dared to treat a girl the way you have treated my Dumpling?

BRINDSLEY: Well, I assume, Colonel—

COLONEL: Hold your tongue, I'm talking!

CAROL: Oh, leave it, Daddy. Let's just go home.

COLONEL: In a moment, Dumpling. Kindly leave this to me.

BRINDSLEY: Look, Carol, I can explain—

CAROL: Explain what?

BRINDSLEY: It's impossible here.

COLONEL: You understate, sir.

BRINDSLEY: Carol, you don't understand.

CAROL: What the hell's to understand? All the time you were going with me, she was in the background—that's all there is to it. What were you doing? Weighing us up? . . . Here! [*She pulls off her engagement ring.*]

BRINDSLEY: What?

CAROL: Your ring. Take the bloody thing back!

[*She throws it. It hits the* COLONEL *in the eye.*]

COLONEL: My eye! My damned eye!

[CLEA *starts to laugh again.*]

[*In mounting fury, clutching his eye.*] Oh, very droll, madam! Very droll indeed! Laugh your fill! . . . Miller! I asked you a question. Do you know what would have happened to a young lout like you in my day?

BRINDSLEY: Happened, sir?

COLONEL [*quietly*]: You'd have been thrashed, sir.

BRINDSLEY [*nervous*]: Thrashed—

125 [*The man of war begins to go after him, feeling his way in the dark, like some furious robot.*]

COLONEL: You'd have felt the mark of a father's horsewhip across your seducer's shoulders. You'd have gone down on your cad's bended knees, and begged my daughter's pardon for the insults you've offered her tonight.

BRINDSLEY [*retreating before the* COLONEL'*s groping advance*]: Would I, sir?

COLONEL: You'd have raised your guttersnipe voice in a piteous scream for mercy and forgiveness!

SCENE 9

[*A terrible scream is indeed heard from the hall. They freeze, listening as it comes nearer and nearer, then the door is flung open and* HAROLD *plunges into the room. He is wild-eyed with rage: a lit and bent taper shakes in* 126 *his furious hand.*]

HAROLD: Ooooooh! You villain!

BRINDSLEY: Harold—

HAROLD: You skunky, conniving little villain!

BRINDSLEY: What's the matter?

HAROLD [*raging*]: Have you seen the state of my room? My room? My lovely room, the most elegant and cared for in this entire district? One chair turned absolutely upside down, one chair on top of another like a Portobello junkshop! And that's not all, is it, Brindsley? Oh no, that's not the worst by a long chalk, is it, Brindsley?

BRINDSLEY: Long chalk?

HAROLD: Don't play the innocent with me! I thought I had a friend living here all these years. I didn't know I was living opposite a Light-fingered Lenny!

BRINDSLEY: Harold!

HAROLD [*hysterical*]: This is my reward, isn't it? After years of looking after you, sweeping and tidying up this place, because you're too much of a slut to do it for yourself—to have my best pieces stolen from me to impress your new girl friend and her daddy. Or did she help you?

BRINDSLEY: Harold, it was an emergency.

HAROLD: Don't talk to me: I don't want to know! I know what you think of me now. . . . "Don't tell Harold about the engagement. He's not to be trusted. He's not a friend. He's just someone to steal things from!"

BRINDSLEY: You know that's not true.

HAROLD [*shrieking—in one hysterical breath*]: I know I was the last one to know—that's what I know! I have to find it out in a room full of strangers. Me, who's listened to more of your miseries in the small hours of the morning than anyone else would put up with! All your boring talk about women, hour after hour, as if no one's got troubles but you!

CLEA: She's getting hysterical, dear. Ignore her.

HAROLD: It's you who's going to be ignored, Clea. [*To* BRINDSLEY.] As for you, all I can say about your engagement is this: you deserve each other, you and that little nit.

[CAROL *gives a shriek.*]

BRINDSLEY: Carol!

HAROLD: Oh, so you're there, are you? Skulking in the shadows!

BRINDSLEY: Leave her alone!

HAROLD: I'm not going to touch her! I just want my things and I'll be off. Did you hear me, Brindsley? You give me my things now, or I'll call the police.

BRINDSLEY: Don't be ridiculous.

HAROLD [*grimly*]: Item: One lyre-back Regency chair, in lacquered mahogany with ormolu inlay and appliqué work on the cushions.

BRINDSLEY: In front of you.

[HAROLD *throws the tapers at it to see it.*]

HAROLD: Ta. Item: One half-back sofa—likewise Regency—supported by claw legs and upholstered in a rich silk of bottle green to match the aforesaid chair.

BRINDSLEY: In the studio.

HAROLD: Unbelievable! Item: One Coalport vase, dated 1809, decorated on the rim with a pleasing design of daisies and peonies.

BRINDSLEY: On the floor.

HAROLD: Ta.

[~~BRINDSLEY hands it to him.~~]

Ooooh! You've even taken the flowers! I'll come back for the chair and sofa in a minute. [*Drawing himself up with all the offended dignity of which a* HAROLD GORRINGE *is capable.*] This is the end of our relationship, Brindsley. We won't be speaking again, I don't think.

[*He twitches his raincoat off the table. Inside it, of course, is the Buddha, which falls on the floor and smashes beyond repair. There is a terrible silence. Trying to keep his voice under control.*]

Do you know what that statue was worth? Do you? More money than you'll ever see in your whole life, even if you sell every piece of that nasty, rusty rubbish. [*With the quietness of the very angry.*] I think I'm going to have to smash you, Brindsley.

127 BRINDSLEY [*nervously*]: Now steady on, Harold . . . don't be rash . . .

HAROLD: Yes, I'm very much afraid I'll have to smash you. . . . Smash for smash—that's fair do's. [*He pulls one of the long metal prongs out of the sculpture.*] Smash for smash. Smash for *smash!* [*Insanely he advances on* BRINDSLEY, *holding the prong like a sword, the taper burning in his other hand.*]

BRINDSLEY [*retreating*]: Stop it, Harold. You've gone mad!

COLONEL: Well done, sir. I think it's time for the reckoning. [*The* COLONEL *grabs the other prong and also advances.*]

BRINDSLEY [*retreating from them both*]: Now just a minute, Colonel. Be reasonable! . . . Let's not revert to savages! . . . Harold, I appeal to you—you've always had civilized instincts! Don't join the Army! . . .

CAROL [*grimly advancing also*]: Get him, Daddy! Get him! Get him!

BRINDSLEY [*horrified at her*]: Carol!

CAROL [*malevolently*]: Get him! Get him! Get . . .

BRINDSLEY: Clea!

128 [CLEA *leaps up* ~~and blows out the taper~~. *Lights up.*]

COLONEL: Dammit!

[CLEA *grabs* BRINDSLEY'S *hand and pulls him out of danger.*]

[*To* CLEA.] Careful, my little Dumpling. Keep out of the way.

HAROLD [*to* CAROL]: Hush up, Colonel. We'll be able to hear them breathing.

COLONEL: Clever idea! Smart tactics, sir!

[*Silence. They listen.* BRINDSLEY *climbs carefully onto the table and silently pulls* CLEA *up after him.* HAROLD *and the* COLONEL, *prodding and slashing the darkness with their swords, grimly hunt their quarry. Twenty seconds pass. Suddenly, with a bang* SCHUPPANZIGH *opens the trap from below. Both men advance on it warily. The electrician disappears again below. They have almost reached it, on tiptoe, when there is another crash—this time from the hall. Someone has again tripped over the milk bottles.* HAROLD *and the* COLONEL *immediately swing round and start stalking upstage, still*

SCENE 10
on tiptoe. Enter GEORG BAMBERGER. *He is quite evidently a millionaire. Dressed in the Gulbenkian manner, he wears a beard, an eyeglass, a frock coat, a top hat, and an orchid. He carries a large deaf aid. Bewildered, he advances into the room. Stealthily, the two armed men stalk him upstage as he silently gropes his way downstage and passes between them.*]

'BAMBERGER [*speaking in a middle-aged German voice, as near to the voice of* SCHUPPANZIGH *as possible*]: Hello, please! Mr. Miller?

[HAROLD *and the* COLONEL *spin round in a third direction.*]

HAROLD: Oh, it's the electrician!

BAMBERGER: Hello, please?

COLONEL: What the devil are you doing up here?

[SCHUPPANZIGH *appears at the trap.*]

Have you mended the fuse?

HAROLD: Or are you going to keep us in the dark all night?

SCHUPPANZIGH: Don't worry. The fuse is mended.

[*He comes out of the trap.* BAMBERGER *goes round the stage, right.*]

HAROLD: Thank God for that.

BAMBERGER [*still groping around*]: Hello, please? Mr. Miller—vere are you? Vy zis darkness? Is a joke, yes?

SCHUPPANZIGH [*incensed*]: Ah, no! That is not very funny, good people— just because I am a foreigner, to imitate my voice. You English can be the rudest people on earth!

BAMBERGER [*imperiously*]: Mr. Miller! I have come here to give attention to your sculptures!

SCHUPPANZIGH: *Gott in Himmel!*

BAMBERGER: *Gott in Himmel!*

BRINDSLEY: God, it's him! *Bamberger!*

CLEA: He's come!

HAROLD: Bamberger!

COLONEL: Bamberger!

[*They freeze. The millionaire sets off, left, toward the open trap.*]

BRINDSLEY: Don't worry. Mr. Bamberger. We've had a fuse, but it's mended now.

BAMBERGER [*irritably*]: Mr. Miller!

CLEA: You'll have to speak up. He's deaf.

BRINDSLEY [*shouting*]: Don't worry, Mr. Bamberger! We've had a fuse,
but it's all right now! . . .

[*Standing on the table, he clasps* CLEA *happily.* BAMBERGER *misses the
trap by inches.*]

Oh, Clea, that's true. Everything's all right now! Just in the nick of
time!

[*But as he says this* BAMBERGER *turns and falls into the open trapdoor.*
SCHUPPANZIGH *slams it to with his foot.*]

SCHUPPANZIGH: So! Here's now an end to your troubles! Like Jehovah in
the Sacred Testament, I give you the most miraculous gift of the
Creation! Light!

CLEA: Light!

BRINDSLEY: Oh, thank God. *Thank God!*

[SCHUPPANZIGH *goes to the switch.*]

HAROLD [*grimly*]: I wouldn't thank Him too soon, Brindsley, if I were
you!

COLONEL: Nor would I, Brindsley, if I were you!

CAROL: Nor would I, Brinnie Winnie, if I were you!

SCHUPPANZIGH [*grandly*]: Then thank *me!* For I shall play God for this
second! [*Clapping his hands.*] Attend all of you. God said: "Let there
be light!" And there was, good people, suddenly!—astoundingly!—
instantaneously—inconceivably—inexhaustibly—inextinguishably and
eternally—LIGHT!

[SCHUPPANZIGH, *with a great flourish, flicks the light switch. Instant
darkness. The turntable of the record player starts up again, and with an
exultant crash the Sousa March falls on the audience—and blazes away in
the black.*]

END

Zusätzliche Regieanweisungen zum Text BLACK COMEDY

1. Brindsley dumps down a chair
2. Brindsley paces nervously
3. Brindsley sits down on the sofa
4. Carol goes to the drinks table downstage left
5. Carol moves over to the sofa, where Brindsley is sitting, and sits next to him
6. Carol's questions are very quick and sharp. Brindsley answers more and more slowly
7. Carol moves to the record player
8. Brindsley moves downstage left, kneels by the drinks table, and raises his arms for prayer
9. Carol walks behind the sofa
10. Brindsley gropes his way to the light switch downstage left
11. Brindsley moves towards the drinks-table
12. Carol moves towards the record player
13. Brindsley feels round the bottles
14. Brindsley moves from the drinks table towards the telephone upstage right, narrowly missing the centre table and the sofa
15. Carol walks up the stairs and disappears behind the curtain.
16. Brindsley gets entangled in the telephone wire
17. Carol re-enters from upstairs
18. Brindsley misses the telephone, disentangles himself from the wire.
19. Miss Furnival's voice off. The audience can see only her hands. Brindsley walks towards the entrance.
20. Enter Miss Furnival
21. Brindsley and Miss Furnival narrowly miss one another. They proceed towards the sofa
22. Brindsley finds Miss Furnival, leads her back to chair 1
23. Miss Furnival sits. Brindsley stands behind the chair
24. Brindsley starts to go towards the telephone
25. Brindsley reaches the phone, dials "0"
26. Brindsley stands behind the phone
27. Brindsley calls to Carol (still upstage centre). Carol moves towards him, very narrowly missing the sculpture. Brindsley hands her the receiver. Brindsley moves towards the exit, bumps into the sculpture

28. Miss Furnival raises her arms in disgust
29. Carol moves towards exit door
30. Enter the Colonel. Stops, looks around. Lighter
31. The Colonel is behind chair 1
32. The Colonel starts crossing the room, slowly. Miss Furnival rises, follows him
33. The Colonel (and Miss Furnival closely behind him) have reached chair 2. The Colonel turns round, moves his head backwards in surprise, then moves it angrily towards Miss Furnival who retreats to the sofa. Miss Furnival eventually sits down heavily. Carol watches all this from the drinks table. The Colonel looks around, satisfied with himself. Sees the sculpture
34. Carol moves to Miss Furnival, pats her shoulders. The Colonel moves to the sculpture
35. The Colonel moves to the budha
36. Carol motions her father to the studio, upstage left
37. Carol sits next to Miss Furnival
38. Carol wildly embraces Miss Furnival, kissing her on the cheek. Miss Furnival is alarmed
39. The Colonel returns, moves behind the sofa
40. Re-enter Brindsley from upstage left
41. Brindsley goes to the sofa, stands to the right of the Colonel
42. The Colonel moves towards Brindsley. Brindsley retreats
43. Brindsley turns, and arrives at chair 1
44. They move back to chair 2
45. Brindsley and the Colonel arrive at chair 2
46. Brindsley and the Colonel arrive at chair 2
46. Brindsley moves towards the exit
47. The Colonel sits in chair 3
48. On Brin's arm, Harold walks through the room
49. Harold and Brindsley arrive near the centre table
50. Brindsley crosses to the Colonel (chair 3), blows out the light
51. Brindsley places the coat on the right-hand side of the sofa. Moves back to the left behind the sofa
52. Brindsley returns to the sofa
53. The Colonel remains in chair 3
54. Carol and Brindsley disappear behind the curtain upstage centre

55. Brindsley and Carol emerge frcm behind the curtain

56. Both are still on the stairs

57. Carol and Brindsley come down the stairs. Carol walks to the drinks-table

58. Brindsley bumps into Harold, at the centre table

59. Brindsley moves to the door

60. Brincsley looks around the room, moves to chair 1

61. Brindsley is behind Harold. Carol blows out the match. Brindsley starts to leave the room

62. Re-enter Brindsley. Places old chair into position 1

63. Brindsley places the chair in position 1

64. Brindsley reaches chair 2

65. Exit Brindsley

66. Re-enter Brindsley, with a rocking-chair. Walks to position 3

67. Brindsley arrives at position 3, right in front of the Colonel

68. The Colonel rises. Brindsley exchanges the chairs. The Colonel moves straight across the room to the centre table. Brindsley, at the same time, moves to the table, too, approaching it from the right. During all this: no dialogue. Brincsley anc the Colonel arrive at the table at the same time, their hands narrowly miss. Brindsley places the bowl under the Table.

69. Brindsley walks to the exit through the arch provided by Carol's and the Colonel's arms. Exit Brindsley. Carol gives a glass of scotch to the Colonel

70. The Colonel goes back to chair 3. Re-enter Brindsley with a regency chair!

71. Brindsley sits

72. Brindsley places the chair in position 2

73. The Colonel sits. Brindsley moves to the sofa, Harold rises

74. Carol is at the drinks table

75. Brindsley finds the lamp, upstage right. Crosses left, past the rocking chair

76. Brindsley tugs at the lamp-wire

77. The Colonel falls, because Brincsley tugs again. Lamp-shade comes off

78. Brindsley crawls across the stage, removes the plug, crawls back, gets entangled. Carol prepares Bitter Lemon and Gin

79. Carol moves to Harold, two drinks in her hands. Gives Bitter Lemon to Harold

80. The Colonel rises, goes to Carol, takes Gin. Brindsley searches for the lamp-shade. Carol sits on the sofa, to the left of Miss Furnival

81. Brindsley starts searching for the Budha

82. Exchange of drinks. The Colonel gives his glass to Miss Furnival. Harold gives his glass to the Colonel. Miss Furnival gives her glass to Harold. During this: Brindsley searches for the lamp-shade

83. Brindsley returns, still entangled in the lamp wire

84. Brindsley moves behind the sofa

85. Harold sits on the sofa, right

86. Miss Furnival sits on chair 1

87. Carol moves to the drinks-table

88. Harold rises, goes to the drinks-table. Clea crosses to the sofa

89. Harold gets his drink. After that, Brindsley and Harold move towards the sofa

90. Clea sits in the middle of the sofa, Brindsley sits right, Harold left

91. The Colonel moves to chair 1, sits down carefully. Harold falls off the sofa, gets up, takes out a brightly coloured handkerchief and brushes his legs, then sits down again

92. Clea rises, remains standing in front of the sofa

93. Clea moves behind the sofa, right

94. Clea has reached the drinks-table, takes the Vodak-bottle

95. Carol moves to the sofa, then to chair 2

96. Brindsley finds Clea, pushes her upstairs

97. Exeunt Brindsley and Clea

98. Miss Furnival goes to the drinks table. The Colonel moves from chair 2 to the drinks-table

99. Miss Furnival returns to the sofa, right

100. Brindsley enters upstairs, tie loosenend, open shirt, messy hair

101. Clea emerges at the top of the stairs, trying to pull Brindsley back upstairs, catching him by the tie

102. Clea disappears again

103. Carol moves from chair 2 to the stairs

104. Enter Schuppanzigh, moves near chair 2. Carol searches for Brindsley

105. Brindsley and Carol move downstage left

106. Schuppanzigh paces his bag, cap, and coat on chair 2.
     Brindsley places the table-cloth across the sofa

107. Brindsley moves back to Schuppanzigh. Carol stands near
     to Schuppanzigh, other side

108. Carol moves close to Schuppanzigh, so does Harold

109. Miss Furnival rises, moves to Schuppanzigh, from behind

110. Schuppanzigh sees the sculpture, moves towards it.
     Brindsley and Carol follow

111. The Colonel rises, moves to chair 3. All the others are
     near Schuppanzigh. Harold is on chair 1

112. All rise, react. The Colonel moves to Schuppanzigh, so
     does Brindsley

113. Schuppanzigh moves to chair 2, followed by Brindsley.
     Schuppanzigh takes his coat, cap and bag

114. Carol ushers Schuppanzigh to the audience level, then
     she moves to the record player

115. Brindsley moves to the stairs

116. Clea moves to the table. Brindsley moves to Carol

117. Harold moves to Clea, centre table

118. Brindsley is near Carol. Clea and Harold move towards
     Brindsley and Carol

119. The Colonel goes to the record player

120. The Colonel moves to the left, to chair 3

121. Carol moves to chair 2

122. Miss Furnival appears from the left

123. Clea moves downstage right

124. The Colonel rises and moves downstage right

125. Clea sits on chair 2

126. Re-enter Harold, lantern instead of taper

127. Harold moves to the statue

128. Clea takes away the lantern

KINDER-, SCHUL- UND JUGENDTHEATER

Herausgegeben von Charlotte Oberfeld und Heiko Kauffmann

Band 1   Charlotte Oberfeld, Heiko Kauffmann: Kinder- und Jugendtheater. WERKSTATTBE-
RICHTE. 1983.

Band 2   Ruth Kayser: Von der Rebellion zum Märchen. Der Etablierungsprozeß des Kinder- und
Jugendtheaters seit seinen Neuansätzen in der Studentenbewegung. 1985.

Band 3   Irene Batzill: Vom Frust zur Selbstbestätigung. Beeinflußt das Jugendtheater die Persön-
lichkeitsbildung? 1986.

Band 4   Daniel Meyer-Dinkgräfe: Englisches Schülertheater - Black Comedy. Theorie und Praxis
einer englischsprachigen Theater-Arbeitsgemeinschaft in der gymnasialen Oberstufe.
1988.